The Most Powerful G⊙AL Achievement System in the World™

The Hidden Secret to Getting Everything You Want

Mike Pettigrew

The Most Powerful Goal Achievement System in the World™
The Hidden Secret to Getting Everything You Want
© 2017 Mike Pettigrew

Published by: Reader's Mind Publishing

Visit the author's website:
www.mikepettigrew.com

Get a Free 4-Part Video Training Program: www.mikepettigrew.com/keys

Cover and Interior Design: Left Coast Design, Portland, OR

Dedication

To Helen, Luke and Alannah for being the centre of my world and the reason for everything that I do. I'm so grateful to have such a wonderful family.

To all the amazing people I've met in my life, as well as the mentors and coaches who have helped me to discover that truly anything is possible when you set your mind and heart on it.

And to my wonderful parents who have taught me the importance of caring for others as well as believing in myself, especially during the most difficult times.

CONTENTS

"To live a fulfilled life, we need to keep creating the "what is next", of our lives. Without dreams and goals there is no living, only merely existing, and that is not why we are here."

Mark Twain

Introduction

Are you happy with your life? I mean really, really happy? Or do you feel that things could be better, possibly even a lot better? Life can be exhilarating, fun, and exciting, or it can be boring, challenging, and full of pain.

Why is it that good things always seem to happen to some people, while others get left far behind? It may seem unfair when you feel trapped by circumstances that appear to be beyond your control, or if everything you try just doesn't seem to work out. It's so easy to become disillusioned, to lose spirit, and to just put up with second best all the time.

Life can be hard, but it doesn't have to be like that. You really can change what happens to you. You can transform your life. You can achieve what you yearn for, and you can become deeply happy and truly fulfilled - providing you do the right things and in the right way.

You see, there is a reason why we don't achieve our goals in life, and why life may seem like an endless painful struggle. In this book you will discover why that is, and more importantly, you will discover how to change your life and achieve your goals in the fastest most powerful way possible. You will discover that rather than being "you are what you eat", really "you are what you think, feel, and do".

You will see how your dominant thoughts, emotions and actions create the circumstances of your life. And when you change your dominant thoughts and emotions, and start taking the right actions, your environment will reflect those changes and your circumstances can improve dramatically.

This is the true secret to long-term success and happiness – if you want to change your circumstances, you must first make a change within yourself. And you will discover that change can be a lot easier than you may think! With the exciting tools, techniques, and strategies that I will share with you in this book, you will find out how to powerfully propel your life forwards in a wonderful new direction, so you can achieve your life's biggest dreams, and become the person you always wanted to be.

What You Will Learn

In this book, you will discover the seven powerful steps in this accelerated goal achievement system. These steps can help you to get whatever you want from life as quickly and easily as possible. You will also find background material supporting each of the steps. This will give you a better understanding of why they work, and how to use them most effectively. You will also come across six "magnifiers" that can significantly speed up all your results.

In the main steps of the system, you will learn:

➤ How to use brainstorming sessions to discover what you really want from life, if you are not already clear.

➤ How to combine and condense your goals, so that they become highly charged and far more powerful.

➤ How to regroup your goals with time limits, so that they are achieved more easily.

➤ How to convert condensed goals into powerful affirmations, that program your subconscious mind to bring you what you want. And how to combine affirmations with cutting-edge technology, so you can speed up the achievement of your goals.

➤ Simple techniques to create highly focussed action plans, that you can use to move towards your goals more quickly.

➤ Powerful high performance techniques to free up your time, give you more energy and focus while reducing stress, so that you can progress all your goals more easily.

➤ How to finally root out and overcome self-limiting beliefs and conditioning that have been sabotaging your success for many years.

2

In the background material you will:

➤ Learn how your beliefs have been created, and how the conditioning you have received throughout your life may be currently stopping you from achieving your goals, and what you can do about it.

➤ See how your self-worth limits your earning potential, and you will discover the only truly effective way to increase your income.

➤ Learn why setting goals is vital to your long-term success and happiness, and how to uncover your deep motivations, so you can achieve all your goals a lot more easily.

➤ See how your dominant thoughts, beliefs, and emotions actually create your life experiences, and the scientific studies that validate this.

➤ Discover how your subconscious mind works, and how it controls your life and what you experience, so you can start using it to create what you want.

➤ Find out about cutting-edge technologies that can help you to reprogram your mind, so you can overcome any negative thinking that may be currently stopping you from achieving your goals.

➤ Learn the common traits of the world's most successful people, so that you can mirror their habits and success in your own life.

The six "magnifiers" that can help you to speed up your results, include the following:

➤ How to create a positive mental attitude so you can achieve your goals more easily, and become deeply happy and fulfilled.

➤ How to increase your brain power through simple health improvements, so you can improve your focus and gain more energy.

➤ Why developing a "persistence mindset" allows you to overcome setbacks and temporary failures, and actually enables you to achieve really big goals.

➤ Why lifelong learning is so important, and how mentors, coaches and mastermind groups can help you increase your capabilities tenfold, and achieve your goal more quickly.

➤ How to discover your own true purpose in life, so that you can make the best use of your time to create a life of continual successes and deep fulfilment.

➤ Ways to access your inner genius, so you can boost your creativity and get answers to any problems from deep within your own mind.

The Power of This System

People often ask me whether this really is the most powerful goal achievement system in the world, and my answer to them is yes, it is. There are many excellent goal achievement systems available, and many of them work well, but in most cases, these systems don't give the actual results that people really want.

How many times have you bought a book or a course that simply ends up on the shelf gathering dust? I believe we have all been guilty of this, and it's such a shame. It's not necessarily that the book or training program has failed us, rather we get discouraged when we don't see results quickly enough. Also, we are living in an age where people's attention span has become very short, and it's easy to become distracted by the next "shiny object" so we miss what's truly important, even if it's right in front of us.

People need results, and they need those results fast, or they tend to give up too easily. Many of the better goal achievement systems available today are simply too complicated or confusing. Some of these have as many as 30 or more steps in the process. That's way too complex for most people! The vast majority of people want simplicity and they need results fast, or they will never truly get started.

Sadly, most goal achievement systems also ignore how important a part beliefs and conditioning play in goal achievement. Negative beliefs and restrictive conditioning are two of the main reasons why people fail to achieve their biggest goals in life.

You have within you, right now, deep seated beliefs about your current abilities, and what you can and cannot achieve. It is this

4

conditioning that is your true enemy, because it stops you from achieving the more important goals in your life. And in this book, I will help you to finally root out and uncover what has been holding you back, and exactly what it is that has been sabotaging your chances of achieving your life's biggest goals.

Likewise, other goal achievement systems often ignore the importance of emotionalising your goals. Goals that are lacking in emotion are as good as dead, and they are far more difficult to achieve. In this book, you will discover ways to infuse powerful emotions into all your goals, so that you can achieve them far more easily and a lot more quickly.

The accelerated goal achievement formula you have in your hands right now provides you with a completely new opportunity, and it is different to all other systems. In this book, you will discover the seven steps to achieving anything you want from life. These seven steps are easy to understand, but more importantly they are simple to put into practice.

So, when you test this system and quickly get proof that it works, then you will start to trust it. And when you start getting even more tangible results, you will be excited and empowered, and you will start to develop deeper confidence in your ability to create the life that you want – even if right now you don't believe it's possible.

Success Is Just Around the Next Corner

With this system, you can start seeing tangible changes within the next couple of weeks, and when this happens your beliefs about what is possible will begin to change. Then, as you stretch your realm of possibility, bigger and bigger goals will naturally come within your reach.

A baby learning to walk takes a few steps, falls down, and tries again. Very quickly, that baby develops confidence and the ability to walk, and later can even start to run. Likewise, when you set a small goal for yourself – a goal that stretches your life just a little more than before — and you then achieve that goal, you will start developing greater confidence in your ability to transform your dreams into reality.

Gradually, as you stretch your life bit by bit, and get even more proof that this system works, you will be able to set bigger and bigger goals, and transform your life in ways that may be completely unimaginable to you right now.

I want to make you a promise, right here, right now. I promise that the content in this book will help you make major transformations in your life, providing you follow the seven simple steps.

Imagine what it would be like to wake up each morning excited, and looking forward to the day ahead. Imagine how it would feel to know absolutely in the core of your being that you can achieve whatever you want. What would it be like if you knew that you could never fail?

How would your life be if you were confident and happy most of the time? What would other people start saying about you when they see you experiencing success after success? They'd want to know your secret, wouldn't they?

As Mahatma Gandhi once said, "Be the change that you wish to see in the world". In this book, you will discover how to change your inner life, so that you can start seeing big changes in the world around you and in what happens to you from this point forwards.

A journey of a thousand miles begins with a single step. I invite you now to take that first step forwards with me, to create a far better future for yourself – a life where you start achieving everything that you truly desire.

You are just about to begin the most exciting and rewarding journey of your life!

An Amazing Discovery
(and why I wrote this book)

At this point, you are probably wondering who is Mike Pettigrew and why is he sharing this information with me? Today, I'm an entrepreneur and bestselling author. I've been interviewed on radio and TV many times, helping people just like you to live happier, more successful lives. I have also started, bought, built, and sold businesses that have made millions.

However, it wasn't always that way. If you turn the clock back some years, my life was a living hell. I had lost everything that I had built up over the previous 20 years. It even got so bad that I didn't have any money to feed my wife or our baby son who had just been born.

Have you ever felt so overwhelmed by fear that it affected you physically? You know that nauseating feeling in the pit of your stomach. It's awful, and paralysing isn't it? And when it also involves your loved ones, it's a terrible shock to the system.

Every morning, I used to waken up shaking with fear. Having to face yet another excruciatingly painful day became almost unbearable. I used to get out of bed and run straight to the toilet, because the fear was so overpowering that I wanted to vomit. And this went on for a very long time. I honestly believe that there is nothing more frightening than a threat to the survival of your loved ones.

The situation I found myself in was a huge shock, because previously I had been very successful. Just a few years earlier, I had sold my first really successful business to a multinational, and at that point I was a millionaire. Little could I have imagined what was in store for us, and by trusting the wrong people and by making some very bad investments, we lost every cent we had in the entire world.

It was all gone, nothing left, nada. Slowly but surely, I moved down a slippery slope, going from someone who had lots of confidence and high self-esteem to completely doubting myself and no longer having any trust in my own abilities. I was a failure, and everything I did seemed to make our situation a lot worse.

No matter how happy or successful we may become, we never truly know what may be around the next corner, or what hard lessons we may need to learn. However, I'm of the firm belief that the major painful experiences of our lives can enable us to grow and become kinder, wiser, richer, and more compassionate human beings. But, there is no guarantee — everything depends on how we react to our circumstances, and the choices that we make.

Our Thoughts and Emotions Shape Our World

Finally, it got so bad that I just couldn't take it anymore. I vowed to the universe that the situation would change. I committed my entire being to transforming our situation no matter what it would take. It can be quite amazing what is possible when we commit to something 100%. When we make a vow to transform a painful situation. It's almost like we have to get to the point of screaming at the top of our voices "No more! I will change this no matter what" before real transformation can occur.

Have you ever been in a situation that slowly got worse? If so, you will know how it feels to just put up with it. It seems almost natural to slowly and gradually sink into feelings of despair and powerlessness by constantly putting up with a painful situation. For me, it happened very slowly as our situation became worse and worse. I didn't even notice how my thoughts and emotions had gradually become more negative with each passing day. I hardly even noticed the difference within me by the time I had no more confidence in myself anymore. It all happened slowly and subtly, as I just continued to put up with everything.

The fact is, we really don't need to wait until things become really painful in order to be able to draw forth great power from within our lives. Since we are so good at just putting up with things, we can forget this immense potential for change that always lies within us. I certainly had forgotten this ability until I made my vow, and as soon as I did this — an amazing thing happened.

As soon as I vowed with every fibre of my being to change our situation, it seemed like my prayer was finally answered. The very next day, I came across an old book written over a hundred years ago, and it was all about the power of gratitude. That book was *The Science of Getting Rich* by Wallace D. Wattles and in it, I learned that gratitude acts like a powerful magnet, drawing into our lives all sorts of benefits. On the other hand, fear, resentment, and complaint can have the complete opposite effect. They prevent good things from happening to us.

This book totally opened my eyes. What I was feeling back then was certainly not gratitude, but rather its complete opposite. I kept thinking *why me? Why do I deserve this?* I almost believed there was no point even trying anymore, because I just kept failing again and again. I was literally locked into a vicious cycle of fear, self-doubt, and despair, and everything I did seemed to make our situation far worse. I felt completely paralysed until I read this incredible book. While reading, I started to realise that many of the things that we were experiencing were the direct result of the dominant thoughts and emotions that I was "transmitting out" into the universe from my mind. This wonderful book made me realise that I urgently needed to change my dominant thoughts and emotions.

Before this deeply painful experience, I had been an optimist and a very positive thinker. I was well aware of my own ability to create whatever I wanted, and I had the confidence and determination to bring my goals to fruition again and again. Reading this book about gratitude, I started to realise just how far I had slipped, and just how deep into the pit of despair I had fallen.

My Crazy Gratitude Experiment

That's when I decided to do a little experiment — an experiment I today call "My Crazy Gratitude Experiment". I decided to reprogram my mind with gratitude, so every 30 minutes of the day I asked myself what my most dominant thought and emotion was during the previous 30 minutes.

As you can imagine, having experienced so much loss and continuing to struggle so desperately, my dominant thoughts and emotions were not particularly positive, to put it mildly. So, every 30 minutes of the day, I replaced those negative thoughts and feelings with gratitude.

At this point, you may wonder how it was even possible for me to feel any gratitude at all when things were so awful. However, as well-known author Bruce Moen once told me, *"If you ever want to return to any state of consciousness you have experienced in the past, then all you need to do is remember what it felt like"*.

Bruce had shared this insight with me a few years earlier, while running a workshop at our home. Bruce is a very gifted researcher into the evidence for life after physical death, and his words were a powerful reminder of what we are truly capable of.

So, in my Crazy Gratitude Experiment, I brought up the memory of a time in the past when I had felt deep sincere gratitude. I focused on that experience, and after a couple of minutes I actually started to feel some gratitude. At first, the effects of doing this did not last very long, and that's why I kept focusing on gratitude every 30 minutes of the day. However, after practicing this for only a few hours, I started to feel very differently for the first time in more than a year, even though we were still in a terrible situation. Then, some amazing events started to happen. Coincidences or synchronicities, which still affect me profoundly to this day, started occurring one after another in rapid succession. As I started to manifest more gratitude in my life, gradually our circumstances also began to improve. It took time for the situation to completely transform, but everything started changing as soon as I moved my mindset from fear and resentment to gratitude and appreciation.

Whenever you are suffering deeply, cannot see any way out of your situation, and have experienced despair for a long time, any change in your feelings can be a great relief. As I started to feel differently, and as I started to see new possibilities in my future, my actions also started to change. As all these new coincidences started occurring in rapid succession, my optimism and positivity started to grow once again. And as I started making different actions, I also started seeing different results, and my confidence, which had previously been badly shaken, also started to grow once again. All these changes started happening as a result of my Crazy Gratitude Experiment.

No matter how difficult your current situation may be, or how urgently you need to experience rapid change, the power of gratitude can propel you forwards in a wonderful new direction, and it can do this fast. It may almost seem like you are "living a lie" for a short time, in order to really get this creative process started - but it's not living a lie. Rather, you are consciously choosing a mindset that is the complete opposite to what you had been experiencing. This really works, and it's extremely powerful.

Three days after beginning my Crazy Gratitude Experiment, my phone rang and I answered it. It was an old competitor on the line, and we started discussing his business, and his exciting recent experiences. However, I was far too ashamed to share with him what I myself had been going through.

During our conversation, he told me that he was getting incredible results from a new form of advertising called Google AdWords. At that point, I didn't know anything about this new form of advertising and I asked him to explain exactly what was happening for him. He told me about the little advertisements that appeared down the right-hand side of the Google search results page, and how he was getting an enormous amount of new business from those advertisements, at very low cost, and how it had completely transformed his business.

That conversation, only three days after I started my experiment had the effect of changing my life in more ways than you could probably imagine. Our entire situation did take time to transform completely, with many months of working long hours, and learning all sorts of new skills in rapid succession. However, everything started to change, as soon as I began my Crazy Gratitude Experiment. Since then I myself have spent millions advertising using Google AdWords in all my businesses, and the results have been phenomenal.

Looking back, I can see why I had to go through such a horrendous experience. The challenges I experienced have taught me just how powerful our mind is. We really can think our way to success or failure, and we are totally responsible for everything that happens to us.

This experience has enabled me to share what I have learned with many people around the world. It has allowed me to pass on what I have discovered, so that other people do not need to make the same mistakes, that I made. It has also allowed me to share powerful strategies, tools and techniques that can allow anyone to transform their circumstances in the fastest way possible.

So, the next time you feel stuck and don't know how to change your situation, make sure you test this Crazy Gratitude Experiment for yourself, and see what happens!

Be the Change You Want to See

No matter what you want to change or achieve in your own life right now, you can do so only when you change what's inside you. You can become bitter, resentful, and disillusioned and thereby experience even more suffering, or you can make a change that will powerfully touch every area of your life. A single positive, powerful, inner change is a bit like pulling the corner of a spider's web. When you pull the corner of the web, the entire web of your life changes shape too. In other words, change just one aspect of your life and your whole life changes as a result!

I'm now very grateful for the painful experiences I went through all those years ago. They have given me far greater strength, new skills I never had before, greater meaning and purpose in my life, and a greater determination to make a difference in the world around me. I honestly believe that when you discover powerful new ways to transform your own life and achieve your biggest goals, then it is your obligation to share what you have learned with others.

I believe that the greatest crime is to learn something that can significantly benefit other people, yet share it with no one. On the other hand, when we transform our lives, change our circumstances, and fulfil our dreams, we simply must share what we have learned with others. If we don't do this, then everything we have gone through has been wasted.

This is the reason why I have written this book, and why I feel so passionate about helping people to become deeply happy and achieve their life's biggest goals.

You are so close to creating the life you have always yearned for and you're in exactly the right place, and it's exactly the right time for you to do so. Because very soon, I will share with you the fastest, most reliable, and easiest way to achieve all your goals in life.

Achieving Your Goals Is Easy

At this point, you may be concerned that this will be a lot of hard work, and while I must admit a certain degree of work is required, it does not have to be painful, and it is definitely worth the effort! You see, there is an easy way to achieve your goals, and there is a hard way. The hard way - the very hard way — is to do nothing at all and hope that your life will improve, which it most likely will not. Or you can use a tried and tested system that will allow you to achieve your goals 10 times faster.

You deserve to achieve your life's biggest dreams in the most direct manner possible, and trial and error really is no longer necessary. In fact, trial and error, or trying to learn everything yourself through direct experience, can be a very big waste of your time. After all, you only have so many hours in each day, days in each week, and weeks in each year to achieve your goals.

Life is simply too short to rely on your own untested methods in the hope that they just might work out. Likewise, if you just keep doing the same things and expect your life to change, then you will be very, very disappointed. In fact, Albert Einstein once said that the definition of insanity was *"Doing the same thing over and over again and expecting different results "*.

You can only achieve your goals in life, when you try new things — but there is no need to reinvent the wheel. When you learn from others how they achieved their goals quickly, it can speed up your own results enormously.

There is a formula for achieving everything you want in life, and it's easy to understand, simple to put into practice, and you can start seeing results right from the start.

The Most Powerful Goal Achievement System in the World™

U nlike other goal achievement systems that are made up of 30 or 40 complex parts, the Most Powerful Goal Achievement System in the World is made up of only seven simple steps. However, if you want to make sure you achieve your goals, and achieve them as quickly as possible, then it is very important that you use each one of these steps correctly.

Please do not skip any of them, as doing so could greatly diminish your results. You owe it to yourself to create a life of abundance, true happiness, and deep fulfilment, and you can only achieve these when you pay attention to each one of the seven steps.

Everything is kept simple, so that it is very accessible, and so that you can start getting great results quickly. These steps are what's most important, and nothing has been left out.

Your first few weeks in this journey are actually the most important, because when you start getting results right from the start, your confidence will build, and you will be more empowered.

This in turn means you can start achieving bigger and bigger goals as your confidence grows and you become more proficient in the system.

The 7 Steps To Getting Everything You Want

STEP 1 - Decide What You Want: If you don't already know exactly what you want, don't worry, because in step 1, you'll find out exactly what you want. You'll do brainstorming sessions that will enable you to set clear goals for each major area in your life.

STEP 2 - Create Highly Charged Goals: In step 2, you will create condensed goals that include a powerful motivating factor. This will help you inject emotional power and energy into every goal that you set.

STEP 3 - Give Each Goal a Deadline: In step 3, you'll regroup you goals into short, medium, and long-term goals, and you'll set a specific deadline for each goal.

STEP 4 - Program Your Mind: In step 4, you'll convert your condensed goals into powerful affirmations that program your mind for success. You'll also learn how to overcome negative thoughts, and use creative visualisation, and other powerful mind programming technologies to speed up the process of achieving every one of your goals.

STEP 5 - Plan for Accelerated Success: In step 5, you'll create highly effective action plans that will help you to move towards each of your goals more quickly. You'll also discover how to use mind mapping and focusing questions, so that you keep moving towards your goals in the fastest, most efficient way possible, while eliminating wasted time.

STEP 6 - Become a High Performer: In step 6, you'll start using the same strategies and habits that high performers use to achieve their goals more quickly. You will also discover how to save time, and accomplish more each day. You will also learn how to reduce stress, and improve your performance in every area of your life. You will discover powerful methods to plan your days, and find out how to dramatically improve your health, energy, and brain power in as little as 2 minutes.

STEP 7 - Overcome Limiting Beliefs: In step 7, you will take back full control of your life again by finally rooting out the negative conditioning that's been holding you back since you were a child. Conditioning that has been preventing you from achieving your life's biggest goals. You will also learn how to overcome that conditioning so that you can achieve all your goals faster and a lot easier.

Magnifiers:

In addition, to these seven steps, you will also find six "Magnifiers" spread throughout this book. These magnifiers can greatly enhance your results.

Not only can they speed up the achievement of your goals tenfold, they can also enable you to become deeply happy and fulfilled, and they can bring a greater sense of meaning and purpose into your life, so that you become truly unstoppable.

You Can Achieve Anything You Want

What do you want from life? I mean, what do you really want to achieve? If I were to wave a magic wand so that anything could be possible, what would it be that you would create for yourself?

Would you like to travel more? Or perhaps lose a few extra pounds, or even start a new career — one that you absolutely love? Do you want to have happier, deeper, and more fulfilling relationships? Or maybe work less hard, make more money, and have more free time?

You can achieve all of these goals, but they won't come about just by accident. There is a recipe for achieving your goals. It's a strict formula that when followed to the letter will allow you to create the ultimate lifestyle, and the life you were born to live.

So why is it that many people don't achieve their goals in life? In fact, a lot of people hate setting goals, and this is because they believe that they might fail. Then if they try and fail, they can become even more disillusioned, feel more disempowered, and doubt themselves even more than they did before. So it's no wonder that goal setting can be an uncomfortable topic.

However, the fact is that unless we set clear, concise goals, we are forever

"We get three wishes. Let's not waste them on something like 'Better coffee in the break room'."

doomed to drifting and reacting to changing circumstances. In the next chapter, we'll go into the reasons why you need to set goals, and in a lot more detail, but for now let's focus on what you want to create in your life.

If you ask any highly successful person whether they just fell into success, you'll find that this is rarely the case. Success is always the result of setting clear goals, planning the journey towards achieving those goals, taking consistent actions, and overcoming all the blocks in your way.

Your Beliefs Have Power

Have you ever considered just how much you hold yourself back? It takes courage and responsibility to admit that you are probably your own worst enemy when it comes to achieving your goals. It's the inner blocks to progress that sabotage most people's chance of achieving their life's biggest dreams. This is because what you believe is possible totally dictates what you can and cannot achieve. If deep down you believe you are unworthy, or not clever enough, or not capable enough, then these beliefs will prevent you from achieving anything really substantial in your life.

I became acutely aware of this a long time ago, as my own low self-worth created my first really big problems in business. This was back in 1990, three years after I started an office plant rental business. The first few years, like most businesses were very difficult — I was on a financial rollercoaster. One month there was plenty of money, and the next month I was almost starving. And as I expected more difficulties, that's exactly what I got!

These cash flow problems were all due to my own low self-worth, and the roots of this problem grew many years before, in childhood. When I was a child I had asthma. This meant that I couldn't run very far, or I would end up coughing, spluttering, wheezing, and even fighting for breath.

My classmates discovered very quickly than I was useless at sports. So, whenever they were choosing who would be on their sports team, I was always the very last choice – the one left standing alone.

Nobody wanted me. In fact, they used to argue over not having me on their team! They used to say things like "*We don't want Pettigrew again, he's useless. No way are we having him on our team!"* I used to hear this again and again and again.

When you constantly hear other people saying negative things about you, you can start to believe them. And the more you

"I think I just solved my cash flow problem."

hear those things, the stronger those beliefs get, especially if there is clear evidence that reinforces those beliefs.

This conditioning from my classmates didn't just affect my ability to play sports. It also had a powerful effect on all areas of my life. In my teens and right into my early 20s, I honestly believed that I was useless at most things. I was clumsy, awkward, and shy, and I often felt out of place and very self-conscious.

My life was dominated by beliefs that I was worth very little and that nobody would want me. I was the sort of guy who would go up to a girl at a dance and stutter and stammer and get rejected every time. It was very painful, and I was acutely aware of how my shyness in particular, was preventing me from experiencing all sorts of wonderful things.

Several years later I started my first real business, and it was in an area in which I had absolutely no experience. I studied electronic engineering at college, and I always really loved science and technology (and I still do!). However, after leaving college I immediately started job hunting. I went around knocking on doors of technology and electronic companies. Quite quickly I was offered three jobs — two of them were in electronics, and the other was in sales. I took the sales job.

For me this was very surprising, as I could never have imagined that I would be involved in the world of business. In fact, I used to tease one of my friends at college because he was studying business, which I thought was incredibly boring! The job that I was offered in sales was as a result of knocking on the door of a telephone company. Their rationale for offering me my first job was that I knocked on their door selling myself, so why not send me out knocking on doors selling their telephone systems?

The reason why I took the sales job was that the pay was far better than the other two jobs I had been offered, and I would effectively be my own boss, and I would also get a company car! So I accepted their offer and got started right away.

Less than two years later, I broke up with my girlfriend, who I had been living with, and I was completely devastated. My work began to suffer, and a few short months later I was fired — from the one and only job I ever had! That year, my life changed in every way imaginable. I lost my first great love, my home, my job, and my self-esteem, which had finally started to grow, albeit slowly.

A Crisis Can Be Your Best Opportunity

Looking back, it would have been almost impossible for me to have imagined what lay around the very next corner. Nine months later, I started my own first real business, selling and renting tropical plants to offices, hotels, banks, and shopping centres, thanks to a small loan given to me by my parents. I got my first contract on the very first day! I could hardly believe it when the new client handed me a cheque for £1,500 without any evidence that I could even install and maintain their plants. Of course, I didn't tell them that it was my very first contract.

This was just before Christmas 1987, and Ireland, where I lived, was in the grips of a deep recession. January came, followed by February and March, and no new sales came in. I start to panic and even broke out in eczema with the worry of what might happen soon.

From April onwards, I started getting a few new contracts here and there, and gradually my very small business started to grow and my contract portfolio increased. I took on my first member of staff the following September, with the deep nagging fear that I might not be able to pay them a regular wage.

Thankfully, my fear was unfounded because my time was freed up to make more sales, and get more new clients. The first few years were a financial rollercoaster, and three years later it was still "hand to mouth" a lot of the time.

At the end of 1990, I was on a training course in Japan, and while I was there I made a deep vow to the universe. I already had a clear vision of what I wanted my business to become. My goal was to have such a high income after the first 10 years of business that I would only need to work two days each week, and that I would be able to spend most of my time doing voluntary work. I achieved that same goal seven years later in 1997, which was exactly 10 years after I started that business.

In 1990, all of this was still far off in the future. But I completely realised that in order to achieve that goal, certain things would have to change. And I certainly needed that change, because of the constant financial rollercoaster that I had been experiencing over the previous three years.

As soon as I returned home from Japan, I immediately hit a brick wall. I discovered an even deeper hole in my finances. The amount of money that was coming in from my clients over the next two months was a lot less than the amount of money needed to pay my suppliers.

How was I going to survive? How was I even going to be able to eat? How could my business possibly get through this? And what could I do to not let my suppliers down? These were just some of the questions I was asking myself, and there appeared to be no workable solution available for any of them.

I even started to make plans to fold up the business, and to live on social welfare instead. I really couldn't see any other way forwards. Then it struck me that if I closed the business without first trying new things, I would have just wasted three years of very hard work — there had to be a better way, and fortunately there certainly was.

You Can't Achieve Big Goals if You Have Low Self-Worth

During that year, I also had a series of experiences that highlighted to me that I had low self-worth. For example, I was wasting money on things that I did not need or value. I didn't really understand that money is an exchange of time and effort spent contributing to other people's lives. So, if you waste your money, you are in effect devaluing your own time.

For the first time, I started to realise in the core of my being that all my money problems were due to the conditioning I had received in school, and when I was a child. For many years, I had believed I was worth very little, and I began to realise that I would have to change this if I wanted to be able to rescue my business.

So, I made a big decision, and it seemed a little crazy, but I really had nothing to lose by trying it. I decided to double all of my prices. It was a risk, because if my clients didn't agree to the massive increase, then I would have no business anymore. On the other hand, if even half of them agreed, then I would make twice as much money for exactly the same amount of work.

So, I wrote a letter to each one of my clients explaining that we had to increase our prices quite dramatically to be able to continue providing them with the same level of service that they had come to expect from us. Amazingly, every single one of those clients agreed to the 100% price increase!

I was astonished, especially when one client told me that he had always felt we were far too cheap for the service we provided. From that point forwards, my business grew rapidly and the profits grew enormously.

I also started doing several other things to improve my self-esteem, and self-value. As a result, I quickly started to discover that I had all sorts of abilities I never knew I possessed. For example, I started composing music even though I still can't play the piano! I also slowly but surely started to speak in front of larger and larger groups of people.

The exciting thing is that when you do challenging new

"The Self Esteem Seminar seems to have helped you"

things, your confidence grows, and so does your vision of what might be possible for your life. Everything starts improving dramatically as soon as you focus on improving your own self-worth, and later in this book, I will share with you powerful new ways you can improve your own self-worth, and your earning potential.

As a result of improving my self-worth, seven years later I had achieved most of my biggest goals in life and had reached the point where I only had to work a day and a half each week. The rest of my time was spent doing voluntary work, and giving back to society in a meaningful way, which was exactly the goal I had set for myself.

I also had an amazing lifestyle, and I travelled the world visiting all sorts of exciting and exotic places. I used to travel every January for between four and six weeks, and whenever I returned home, my business would still be thriving, due to the system I had created that allowed me to run my business on virtual autopilot.

By the time 2001 came around, I was a millionaire, and towards the end of that year I sold my business to a multinational. I clearly remember one day that year when it suddenly struck me that I had finally achieved all my life's biggest goals, yet I was still only in my thirties.

The Magic Is Within You

I assure you, I'm a very ordinary person just like you, and if I can do it, you certainly can too. I have gone from rags to riches, and from having very little self-worth to achieving my life's biggest dreams.

What you believe to be possible for you really does determine everything. This is exciting stuff, because it can change the very fabric of your existence, and all the experiences that you attract into your life from this point forwards. You really are what you believe!

Whatever you want from life, it's possible to achieve — providing you are determined to make it happen, and willing to learn new things. In this book, you'll discover a clearer strategy to achieve all your goals — an exciting new system that will allow you to root out and overcome all the blocks to your progress. With this book, you can finally turn your dreams into reality and create the life you have always wanted.

The magic to make all of this happen resides in your own mind, and step by step you will learn how to harness that magic, so you can transform your life and achieve all your goals, faster than you may have ever dreamed possible.

The first step to making all of this happen is to set a goal for yourself – because a goal creates forward thrust and momentum in your life. When you set a goal, it immediately creates change and sets in motion a series of events that move you forwards to a happier and more fulfilling life.

Summary:

> ➤ **You can achieve anything you want** — Providing you set clear goals, and follow a specific formula that will bring them to fruition, you can achieve anything.

> ➤ **Your beliefs have power** — What you believe completely determines whether you can achieve your goals. Fortunately, you can change your beliefs!

> ➤ **A crisis could be your best opportunity** — Facing and overcoming setbacks gives you the power and resources to achieve any goal. They act like a springboard to success.

> ➤ **You can't be rich if you have low self-worth** — Your self-worth determines your earning potential. Improve it and your finances can improve dramatically.

> ➤ **The magic is within you** — You already possess everything within you that you need to become highly successful. You can achieve your goals by using this powerful system.

Why Set Goals?

Many people hate setting goals, because secretly they believe that they may fail to achieve them. Other people are perfectly happy never setting goals, because they believe that their life is just fine the way it is. To others, it may appear that setting goals only puts them under unnecessary pressure and stress.

However, people who consistently set and achieve goals understand that when they set a new goal, they are in fact creating a better life for themselves. They are making a powerful new cause — the effect of which can be more fulfilment and happiness in their life.

There is a big difference between people who set goals and those who never do. The lives of people who regularly set goals can often turn out very different to those who don't set any goals for themselves.

What Happens When You Don't Set Goals

John was frustrated with his life. Really, really frustrated. He was trapped in a dead-end job that he hated, with very low pay. Nobody appreciated him, and life just seemed to be passing him by.

On the third Thursday of every month, John and his old-school friends would always meet up at the local pub. Most of his friends seem to be doing really well, and appeared to be happy. They were all married, or at least in long-term relationships, and most of them had kids too. John had none of these things in his own life. John was cynical, and believed that other people had all the luck and that he had none. Meeting his friends was always embarrassing, and often it was something he dreaded, even though he wanted to spend time with them. His friends would often share all the wonderful things happening in their lives. One of them had travelled the world, three of them had successful businesses, and one had even retired when he was only 35 years old.

John secretly believed there was something wrong with him, something very wrong, but he couldn't quite put his finger on exactly what was. He was lonely, frustrated, and disillusioned. John expected nothing to change, and nothing did change for him. On top of all this, he constantly experienced disappointment after disappointment. Relationships that went wrong after only a short time, a career that never really started, and he seemed to experience constant limitations in everything that he did.

John didn't understand that he too could have experienced all sorts of wonderful things in his life, if only he had done one thing – set clear goals. But John never made any goals. Or more accurately, he hadn't made a concrete goal since he was 11 years old. You see, when he was still just a young boy he had a passion for football. He lived and breathed football every waking moment of his day. He was a good player, but not exceptional because he didn't practice quite as much as some of his teammates.

Around this time, his dad gave him a book about the world's greatest football heroes and it was his prized possession. In this book, he read the experiences of his heroes, and how many of them went from failure after failure to gradually becoming the world's greatest players. All fired up, John made a big decision. He was going to be just like them. He was going to become a football superhero! John started to train more than ever – a lot more. In fact, he trained so much that even his friends began to believe he was going to become the best footballer the school had ever had.

Then John became ill. And what started out as a minor illness quickly developed into something that meant he had to spend 3 months in hospital. John eventually overcame his illness and returned to school. However, he was deeply shocked when he discovered that his team had won the championships without him.

When John was strong enough, he returned to the playing field only to discover that he was no longer on the team! His replacement was getting all the praise for the championships win. John was very unhappy and he grew resentful and bitter. This was the first great setback in his life. Unfortunately,, he allowed this first mishap to dictate how his life would eventually turn out.

"I just go where the bike takes me"

John never made another clear goal from that day on. His belief was that should he fail again, it would be far too painful for him to bear. He built up a skin of protection around himself, but this also prevented good things from happening to him. Eventually, John became a drifter, because he never set any concrete goals, and he only reacted to circumstances as they happened. He never looked forward into the future, and always settled for second best.

On the other hand, his old school mates who were successful, and who seemed to be happy, had not allowed temporary setbacks to prevent them from achieving their life goals. As a result, all of them were able to create some degree of success, happiness, and wealth.

Take Control of Your Life

Sadly, the world is filled with people just like John. They allow fear, lack of understanding, and temporary setbacks to stop them achieving their life's biggest dreams.

For example, many people set big a goal, but are scared of failing, or of the challenges they might have to face to reach that goal. Others don't take any of the right actions to bring their goals to fruition. When this happens, they can end up disillusioned because their goal seems as far away as it did before they even started.

On the other hand, many set a goal, create action steps to achieve that goal, but then give up at the first real setback, justifying to themselves that it probably "wasn't meant to be" anyway.

What all these people fail to realise is that achieving their goals is a lot easier than they might imagine. In order to achieve any worthwhile goal, you just need to follow a simple time-tested formula that works, and follow it to the letter.

The fact is, unless you set specific goals and work towards the achievement of those goals, your life can start to drift. You can end up drifting from one event to another, just reacting to external circumstances, instead of carving out a great future for yourself – a future that you really want.

Unless you set goals, and take the right actions to achieve those goals, you could even grow disempowered. This is because life without goals can become monotonous and unfulfilling, and if you don't set goals, it could even mean that you never discover what you are truly capable of, always settling for second best.

An empowered person is a person who creates real change in their world, whereas a person who is disempowered can achieve very little and constantly faces feelings of dissatisfaction and disappointment.

In one sense, a goal is just a goal, unless you do something about it. On the other hand, when you create a clear, concise goal, and start taking the right actions, it creates forward momentum in your life. Simply put, goals will stretch your life — they will cause you to grow in ways that wouldn't have been available to you before.

Therefore, when you set a goal, it will cause you to make changes in your life – changes that you would not have made otherwise. When you set a goal, you push yourself to develop new skills, seek new experiences, challenge yourself, change your beliefs, and meet new people.

Gateway to a Far Better Life

So, imagine if John had set himself the goal of improving in football, so that he could achieve his dream of becoming a professional footballer. To achieve his goal, he could have developed new footwork skills, sought new types of fitness training, challenged himself to beat his previous records, and found people who are at the top of their game.

Goals cause you to stretch your life beyond its current limitations. The fact is, when you change, your circumstances will also change. If you do not change inside, then your external reality cannot change either.

Setting goals means you are taking control of your life, your destiny, your journey, and also your happiness. Even the act of setting a goal means you are taking control of your own future rather than leaving it up to fate, luck, or the will of others.

Setting goals is your one true guarantee of achieving a far better life for yourself. A life that is exciting, enriching, and rewarding in every way imaginable.

My own experience of setting goals is that my goals have caused me to do all sorts of things that I would never have considered doing otherwise. My biggest goals have made it necessary for me to learn new skills, try new things, and take steps to overcome my own self-limiting beliefs — and it's exactly the same for you too.

Setting goals will cause you to gain new skills, experiences, and positive empowering beliefs. By doing each of these things, you can start to achieve your goals. You can only achieve your goals when you change your life, both internally and externally, and it's not nearly as difficult as you may have believed!

Summary:

> **Goals determine your future** — The lives of people who set goals can turn out very differently to those who do not set goals.

> **Without goals, your life can drift** — You can end up just reacting to changing circumstances, becoming disempowered and disillusioned with life.

➤ **Goals allow you to live a better life** – By setting goals, you can discover what you are truly capable of, and have a much bigger impact on others.

➤ **Goals help you to overcome your limitations** — Goals allow you to create forward momentum in your life. They also enable you to create the life that you want.

➤ **Goals empower you** – They can enable you to become more capable, empowered, happy, successful, and fulfilled.

Discover What You Really Want

S o now you know why it's vital to set goals. But do you actually know what your goals are and what you really want in your life? I mean, if I asked you to tell me all your goals for the next 5 years, would you be able to rattle them off in just a few seconds?

Most people can't do this, because they don't exactly know what they want. And if you're not sure what it is that you want, chances are you may drift and not achieve very much.

This is understandable, especially when you consider that we are living at a time in history when life is incredibly hectic. By the end of the day, you may be totally exhausted, and the last thing you wish to do is plan your life's goals.

Then, by the time the weekend rolls around, you may be so exhausted that thinking about your life's biggest dreams is very far from your mind. Life can be hard, and when you've had many disappointments along the way, it may be difficult to believe that you can really can achieve all those dreams you had as a child.

The great thing though is that it's very easy to discover what you want to achieve in your life, even if right now you're not sure what you want. When you know what you want from life, you're much more likely to achieve it. Many people know exactly what they want, and achieve their goals as a result. In a moment, I will share with you a simple technique that will help you to quickly uncover the goals that will be most meaningful to you.

Disappointments and Setbacks

It's rather sad that by the time many people reach their late 20s, they have had so many disappointments and setbacks, they literally close down their own ability to dream big.

There can be a big difference between someone who is 15 years old and someone who is 30. Often when we are still young, life can seem full of amazing possibilities, and we can be excited about the future. Yet 15 years later, we may have had the stuffing literally knocked out of us by the harsh realities of life. Careers that went wrong, relationships that didn't turn out as we expected, illnesses, and all sorts of other disappointments. This is all a part of growing up and learning that life is not always a bed of roses.

Our challenges can enable us to become wiser, stronger, and more capable individuals, or they can cause us to become disappointed, disempowered, and disillusioned by life. Have you ever felt this way yourself? I imagine you probably have, as most people do at some point in their lives. In fact, my own experience is that most of the people I have met over the years feel disempowered and disillusioned by life to a very significant extent.

It is these disappointments that condition us to expect even more challenges in the future. And sadly, we often experience what we believe may happen. In step seven, you will learn powerful new ways to overcome your self-limiting beliefs, so that you can start dreaming big again, and start making exciting plans again for your future. For the moment, let's look at where you are right now. If you know exactly what it is that you want to achieve, I congratulate you because you are one of the very few who knows what they desire. On the other hand, if you're like most people, you may not know exactly what you want — you're probably not consciously aware of all your life's biggest goals. However, I'm happy to say that you can fix this, and it's so simple that you may even wonder how you never thought of it before.

Do This Exercise: Discover What You Want from Life

To start figuring out what you really want from life, do this simple exercise.

Step 1: If you want to discover what you really want from life, all you need to do is look at your life right now and write down all the things in your life that cause you to suffer. All the things that create pain for you on some level. They could include such things as your relationships, your career, your income and finances, your health, your family, your current abilities, your weight, your emotions, your level of happiness, and a wide range of other issues.

As human beings, we are all very similar, and therefore I am pretty certain that there are many things in your life right now that you are not particularly happy about — things that you really do want to change.

Step 2: The next step is to convert those problems into concrete goals. All you need to do is convert each one into its complete opposite. For example, if you always seem to experience unhappy relationships, then you can create a goal to start having deep, fulfilling, lasting relationships from now on. On the other hand, if you find your career unfulfilling and you're yearning for a change, then it's easy to create a powerful new goal that by say six months from now, you'll be working in a job that you will find both exciting and deeply fulfilling.

Likewise, if you always seem to be broke at the end of each month, or if you are unhealthy, or dissatisfied with any area of your life, you can easily create goals to achieve the opposite of what you are currently experiencing. Simply for the very reason that you are currently suffering from each of these areas of life means you can transform them into goals that are very powerful — goals that will motivate you to create the change that you want to see.

It's really quite simple, isn't it?

> Absolutely **anything that has been causing you to suffer**, especially if it's been going on for a long time, **can be converted into its opposite to create a powerful new goal.**

Here is a process chart to clarify the exercise:

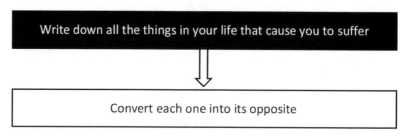

At this point, you may believe that it's impossible to change, particularly if the problem has been going on for a very long time, or that it may be too difficult to transform. Since it's never changed before, why would you even consider that it might change in the future? It's almost natural to be pessimistic, especially when you seem to have all the evidence to validate that it's impossible to change.

As Henry Ford, creator of the first automobiles once said: *"Whether you think you can, or you think you can't - you're right."* I love this saying, because it's so true. Many people hold themselves back enormously because of what they believe. However, in step seven you will discover some very powerful tools and techniques that you can use to overcome this conditioning — and this conditioning is definitely holding you back, right now!

You will learn ways to once again open up your belief in the possibility of a great future. We will work together to bring you back to the point that you were in childhood, where you truly believed anything was possible, where you were excited about the future, and where you could hardly wait to get started.

Let me reassure you, you can achieve virtually anything that you want in your life, providing you set clear goals, take the right actions, and start using the strategies and tools that you discover from the next chapter onwards.

Wants and Needs

In Napoleon Hill's classic book *Think and Grow Rich*, he explains the importance of summoning up a deep burning desire to achieve your goals. This is because **desire is a powerful propelling force for change.**

We all have desires, and desires can be highly motivating, but desires can also get completely out of control, and they can literally drive us in ways that are detrimental to us. A deep desire to help other people can literally change the world. On the other hand, the constant desire for more and

"Hold on, I need that oil for my saute."

more money, and material possessions, can be very destructive and completely unfulfilling.

Desire can be a very powerful creative force, and without it we could not live. It is desire that makes you get out of bed in the morning, to eat, sleep, and work to pay for everything that you consume, and to look after your loved ones. Even your ability to watch a movie, to read, relax, or to listen to music is a fruit of your desire.

Your entire life is the expression and reflection of your desires. Desire in and of itself is neither positive nor negative. It's completely up to you whether it becomes creative or destructive.

To avoid it becoming destructive, you need to understand the difference between what we want and what we need for our happiness and well-being. You need to realise that **needs** are completely different from **wants**. There are all sorts of things we truly *need* in our life. We need food, clothing, shelter, fulfilling relationships, security, exciting new experiences, and a whole range of other things.

A need is something that we must have in order to live in a way that enables us to truly enrich our lives and that may also possibly contribute to other people's happiness. It's something that's not necessarily emotional, but it supports our life at a very deep level.

Wants are things that you don't truly need—things you could survive without or that don't make you truly happy. For example, you may want a big house, expensive cars, and a life of abundance and endless free time. *However, do you honestly need these things to be truly happy?* If you achieve goals such as these, there is no guarantee you will find any of them truly fulfilling.

"He refuses to change the lightbulb until we change"

For example, you might want to work far less and have twice the income. You could have this desire so that you can free up your time and have the money to travel the world and experience new things. This is a really great desire and one that can definitely contribute to your long-term growth, happiness, and fulfilment. On the other hand, you may have exactly the same desire because you hate your work, or simply because you are lazy, and you prefer to do as little as possible.

I discovered this myself a long time ago when I started to taste the material benefits of success. I started spending a lot of money on top of the range cars and all sorts of fun "toys". At first, they made me *feel* successful, but quite quickly I realised that I didn't actually need those things to have that feeling of success inside. I discovered that the excitement of having such things didn't last very long. In fact, I found that they didn't contribute much to my life or my happiness in any meaningful way.

You can feel rich and successful right now without having any trinkets to prove to yourself that you are rich and successful. Now, please don't get me wrong; I'm not saying that you should pretend to be rich and successful, when you may not be so at this moment. I'm definitely not saying "fake it until you make it", as that could make you go broke quite quickly!

What I am saying here is that it's important to start working on overcoming low self-esteem and gradually **improving your self-value**.

The amazing thing is that when you do this, your environment will start reflecting that inner change, and you will encounter external opportunities that will enable you to improve your finances, and increase your material benefits.

So, whenever you create any really big goal for your life, it's important to **discover your Big Why** – the true underlying reason why you want to achieve that goal, and to be deeply honest with yourself. When you uncover your Big Why, you will have an awesomely powerful motivating force that can drive your life in exactly the direction that you both want and need.

When you desire something, it's important to ask yourself *whether you really need that thing, or whether you just want it?* Try to figure out whether you're just avoiding some form of inner change or lack of self-esteem. You need to ask yourself — *do you need it in order to achieve something truly worthwhile, and something that can also contribute to the happiness of others?*

It's always really helpful to look at your desires in this way, especially if you are creating really big goals for your life. So, when you think you want something, or when you're setting your goals, remember to ask yourself do you really need it, or do you just want it to avoid something else?

Do This Exercise: How to Discover Your Big Why

If you'd like to know whether you just *want* something or if you really *need* it to achieve your life's overall plan, this is an exercise that can be very revealing.

Write out each of your goals and add the words "so that" after each one. Next, fill in your reason after the words "so that", and this will bring you even deeper. Keep on going deeper by adding more "so thats" until you discover your single motivating reason for your goal.

Example goal: To work half the time for twice the income…
> ➤ So that: I have more free time, and I can do whatever I want
> ➤ So that: I can learn new things and experience more of life
> ➤ So that: I can discover what I like doing best
> ➤ So that: I can start spending more of my time doing things that I love

> ➤ So that: I can experience more excitement and passion most of the time
> ➤ So that: I can live my life to the fullest
> ➤ So that: I can be deeply happy and truly fulfilled
> ➤ So that: I can be a positive influence on others
> ➤ So that: They can also achieve their goals and become happy too

Big Why for this goal: In this case, your goal could be to work less, make more money, and have more free time, so that you can help others also achieve their goals and become happy too.

Here is a process chart to clarify the exercise:

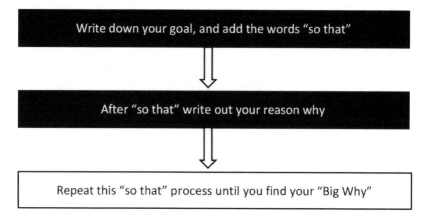

When you drill down through each of your goals like this and get to the Big Why, you will become filled with a deeper sense of purpose, connection, energy, and passion. It's these feelings that we are after here, because they will help you enormously in transforming your goals into reality — in the fastest way possible. A goal that is fuelled with a burning desire or powerful motivating force behind it is truly unstoppable!

On the other hand, after doing this exercise, you may find that some of your goals don't really have a Big Why at all, and they are not as meaningful as you at first believed them to be. You may discover that these goals are just helping you to avoid something you don't really want to face.

You need to make sure you do this exercise fully, because it can help you to avoid wasting a lot of time and energy on goals that are not as important as you at first believed them to be. It can also enable you to inject a lot of passion and energy into goals that you discover are truly worthwhile, and this will greatly speed up your ability to achieve them.

Summary:

> **Knowing exactly what you want is important** - When you know what you want, you are far much more likely to achieve it.

> **You have been conditioned** - Your disappointments and setbacks have conditioned you to expect a mediocre life. What you expect then limits what you can achieve.

> **Discovering what you want is easy** - Write out a list of all the dissatisfactions and frustrations in your life. Converting these into their opposites can create powerful goals.

> **Wants and needs** - You may want something because it enables you to avoid something you don't wish to face, whereas a need is something that can truly improve your life.

> **Your Big Why** - By using the Big Why technique, you can drill down to discover the single underlying motivation behind each of your goals.

STEP 1: Decide What You Want

In the chapter named "Why Set Goals?", I mentioned how important it is to become clear about what you want. Therefore, **the first step in achieving any goal is knowing exactly what you want.**

Unfortunately, many people are not very clear about what they want from life. Life is busy, and few people make the effort to set aside time to plan their lives fully. However, this is crucial, especially if you want to live a life of deep meaning and purpose — and achieve all sorts of wonderful things from now on.

If you are still not clear on what you want to achieve, then it's well worth looking at all the things in your life right now that cause you some form of dissatisfaction or suffering, as we considered earlier.

For example, you may be disappointed and frustrated with your job, your relationships, or the fact that you are always working and never seem to have free time.

You may also be disappointed with your health, your weight, the fact that you never go on holiday, or you may be faced with all sorts of difficult and painful problems. However, it is possible to change all of these things when you set your goals the right way and take consistent daily action.

As you saw earlier, anything at all that causes you to suffer can be converted into a powerful goal — a goal that is the complete opposite of what you have been experiencing. There is nothing quite like exploring your dissatisfactions in life to help you to come up with crystal clear goals — into which you can inject a burning desire for their achievement.

A lack of clarity is responsible for all sorts of disappointments in life. If you aren't very clear about what you want, then it's possible that you may drift through life just reacting to circumstances. We've all seen cases of people drifting through life, achieving very little, and being deeply unhappy and disillusioned. In most cases, this is the result of a lack of clear direction. People who have very little desire in their lives generally achieve very little.

In the Far East, some ancient philosophies focused on extinguishing desires, because it was believed that by extinguishing their desires, people would stop suffering. However, if you look at this more deeply, you will discover that desire is a vital and fundamental aspect of all human life.

If you eradicate desire, then you would not last very long in this world! It is the basic desires for food, warmth, shelter, clothing, and sex that enable the human species to continue. If you successfully overcame desire, then you would waste away quite quickly. So, strong desire is absolutely essential to survive in this world, and it is also a vital element in bringing all your goals to fruition.If you take the time to study the world's most successful people, you will find that in almost every case, their success started with a crystal clear, concise goal that was fuelled by desire — a goal that they felt very strongly about, and that excited them. As I mentioned earlier, unless you feel emotionally connected to your goals, they can be powerless and difficult to achieve.

Therefore, the very first step in achieving any goal is to become clear on exactly what it is that you want, and to have a strong desire to achieve it.

Do This Exercise: Goal Brainstorming Session

To become clear about what you want, simply write out a list of all the things you would like to achieve during your lifetime. It doesn't matter what order you write them in — what's important is that you write down as many goals as you can possibly think of.

It's okay to cross goals off your list later if you find that they're not particularly important to you, or if you don't feel emotionally connected to them. Also, remember to create goals for each major area of your life so that nothing important is left out.

Create goals for each major area of your life:
- ➤ Financial goals
- ➤ Career / business goals
- ➤ Relationship goals
- ➤ Family / free time goals
- ➤ Health / appearance goals
- ➤ Personal growth goals

Here is a process chart to clarify the exercise:

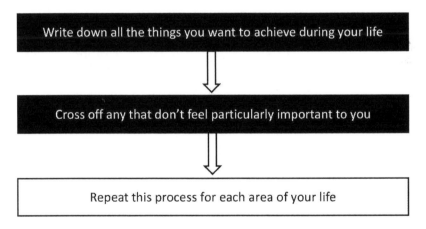

This brainstorming session is very important, so please do it thoroughly and don't rush it. You may even want to have several brainstorming sessions like this, spread over a week or more. The most important thing is that you come up with lots of things that you would like to achieve at some point in your life.

Summary:

➤ **It's important to know exactly what you want** – To become very clear about what you want to achieve, you need to know what you want.

➤ **Goal brainstorming sessions** – Write out all the goals you want to achieve during your life. If necessary, do several sessions over a week or more.

➤ **Create goals for each major area of your life** - Including your finances, career, relationships, recreation, health, and personal growth.

Your Mind Creates Your Experiences

In the introduction to this book, I said that instead of being "you are what you eat", it would be more accurate to say that "you are what you think, believe, and feel".

This is because what you think, believe, and feel affects all your

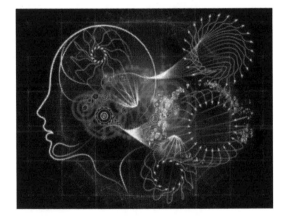

actions, and your actions affect the results you experience in life. You can waste a lot of time and energy running around trying to change your external circumstances, but if you don't transform your inner life, then your results may be a lot less than you'd hoped for.

When you change how you think, what you believe to be true, and how you feel most of the time, you truly have the power to steer your life in any direction that you wish and to achieve the life you yearn for.

This book is all about using concentrated emotion to create powerful changes in the external world, so in this chapter, you'll be able to try experiments that show this is possible. When you discover this truth for yourself, through experimentation, you will also discover the amazing creative force that lies within you, and that can greatly speed up the achievement of all your goals.

Can Your Mind Affect Your Environment?

The idea that our mind affects our environment is not new. For example, an ancient tradition from the Far East tells us that at any moment in time, we are affecting our environment in 3,000 different ways. These ancient texts tell us, for example, that when we are full of anger, this anger is transmitted out into our environment in 3,000 different ways, at every single moment, for as long as we are experiencing that anger.

We may already be aware that when we are feeling deep anger, it affects the colour of our skin, the expression on our face, our movements, the tone and volume of our voice, the temperature of our skin, and also the actions that we take.

However, these ancient writings tell us that our anger actually affects our environment far more profoundly than we may ever be aware of. If this is true, it means that you may need to become more conscious of your dominant thoughts and emotions, because their energy could also affect your experiences.

Science also tells us that energy can neither be created nor destroyed, but that it can only move from one form into another. For example, if we hit the wall with our fist, the energy of our moving fist is transferred into the wall as vibration. Science explains how that energy is never destroyed, but rather it is transmitted out into the universe with infinite effects. My understanding is that emotional energy too can be transmitted out from our life to affect our environment far more powerfully than we may have ever considered.

For example, I attended a meeting several months ago. During that meeting, I was sitting beside someone who I had never met before, and very quickly it felt like a dark cloud had come down over me. I was in great form, but very quickly after sitting beside this person, I started to feel their pain very acutely.

Outwardly, this person just looked quiet and reserved, and she said almost nothing. However, I quickly became aware of the deep emotional pain she was experiencing. It was only later that I got verification of the pain and suffering that she was going through.

Sometimes, when we suddenly experience a strong feeling while in the company of another person, it might mean that we are simply feeling the strong emotions that that person is currently experiencing.

Could it be that strong emotion, just like any form of energy can be "transmitted out" from our life like a radio beacon? Through my own experiences, I believe that it can.

The Power of Emotionalised Thoughts

I often think that strong emotion works a bit like the battery in a cell phone. If our battery is dead, we cannot use our cell phone to speak with someone in the next house, but if our battery is fully charged, then we can use our phone to speak with anyone, anywhere in the entire world.

My experience is that strong emotions literally transmit our desires out into the universe in a very powerful way. Strong desire can achieve anything, whereas a weak will can achieve very little, other than frustration, disempowerment, and disillusionment.

Gone were the days of emotional restraint.

From my own experiences, I have discovered that our thoughts, emotions, and physical state can actually influence people on the other side of the world. Distance seems to be no object.

Many years ago, I was deeply involved in alternative medicine and healing work, and I have spent most of my life studying the mind and the nature of human consciousness. I have had many extraordinary experiences that have proved to me beyond any doubt that our mind really does affect our physical environment in very powerful ways.

One day, I received a telephone call from a relative. He was on a skiing holiday, and he had a chronic sinus infection. In fact, he was in complete agony, but there was no doctor available. He is normally quite sceptical, but he was desperate. He asked whether there was anything that I could do to help him, even though he was thousands of miles away. Calling me for help really was his last resort, but he had nothing to lose in asking for my assistance.

I asked him to hold on the line for a few minutes, while I tried something that might help him. I simply focused my mind and positive emotions on him, particularly around the area of his sinuses, where he was feeling intense pain. After less than a minute, he suddenly said *"What the hell is happening?!"* and I asked him what he meant.

He explained that suddenly he felt his sinuses "opening up", and all the pain had completely disappeared. He was deeply shocked, that it was possible to affect another person over such a very long distance, so powerfully and so quickly. To be perfectly honest, I wasn't at all surprised because I had experienced this sort of thing many times before.

Now, this is just my own personal experience about the power of the mind, and how it can influence other people, which you may or may not believe. However, in recent years scientists have also discovered that the outcome of some sensitive experiments can be powerfully influenced by the observer of those experiments.

Sensitive Experiments Influenced by The Mind

This is particularly evident at the subatomic level, where it has been clearly shown that the observer actually influences the sub atomic particles being observed.

"Is my mind affecting zis book, or is zis book affecting my mind?"

Researchers at the Weizmann Institute of Science conducted a highly controlled experiment that demonstrated how a beam of electrons was affected solely by the act of being observed. This experiment showed that the greater the amount of "watching," the greater the observer's influence on what actually takes place.

Many scientists have validated this and other similar phenomena, for example researcher Dr Masaru Emoto from Japan. Several years ago, Dr Emoto conducted thousands of experiments into the crystallisation of water while that water was starting to freeze. Emoto discovered a fascinating and rather thought-provoking phenomenon. He found that the shapes of freezing water crystals would vary dramatically depending on the thoughts and emotions of the experimenters.

In experiments that he replicated again and again, he discovered that his water samples would crystallise into very specific and beautiful geometric shapes when feelings of love, compassion, gratitude, and a wide range of higher emotions were focussed on those water samples.

On the other hand, he discovered that negative emotions, like envy, hate, anger, and fear produced water crystals shapes that were stunted and ugly. In fact, he discovered that it wasn't just emotion that affected the formation of very definite patterns. Words themselves also had power to affect the creation of specific patterns, again and again.

Massuro Emoto's book "The Hidden Messages in Water" is thought-provoking, and it could explain the mechanics behind all sorts of interesting "new" forms of science and medicine; for example, homeopathy.

When we consider that our body is made from more than 70% water, we should ponder just how powerfully our mind affects our own physical body. It is already a well-known scientific fact that our thoughts, emotions, and perspective can make us ill, or greatly improve our health and well-being.

This Japanese researcher may have also shown that our mind does indeed affect our physical environment, just like the ancient traditions tell us. However, Emoto is not the only researcher or scientist who has been involved in such fascinating research.

Energy Fields and the Mind

During my life, I have had the great privilege of learning directly from some truly exceptional individuals. People who have had an enormous effect on my understanding of life, and what is possible for us as human beings. One of these people is Dr Harry Oldfield, from the United Kingdom. Harry is a renowned scientist and researcher and he is also the inventor of several ground-breaking new technologies, some of which have been featured on the Discovery Channel.

Science from the Far East has recognised for thousands of years that all living organisms possess an energy field, which is partly electromagnetic in nature. Also, that energy travels around the human body along very specific pathways known as meridians. It is these meridians that Chinese medicine and acupuncture use to treat imbalances and numerous illnesses of the body and mind.

Truth of this theory can be demonstrated using Kerlian Photography, which uses high voltages to photograph the energy field around living organisms. For example, it's possible to see the energy field around a leaf. It is also possible to tear off a section of the leaf, and still see the energy field remaining intact where the torn piece of leaf had existed before it was removed.

Many years ago, Harry Oldfield had been conducting his own experiments with Kerlian photography, when he suddenly had an idea. Harry realised that it just might be possible to reveal the energy field around human beings, using simple technology. As a result, Harry developed a remarkable device which he named the PIP Scanner. PIP stands for Poly Contrast Interference Photography, and its principle is quite straightforward.

Using a full spectrum white light, and a regular video camera connected to an ordinary computer running specialised software, it's possible to view the energy field around any living organism, in real time, in full colour on a computer monitor. I've been very fortunate to have trained with Harry Oldfield myself. I also have a Pip Scanner, and it has allowed me to conduct my own experiments into the nature of the mind and how it affects physical matter.

With my own Pip Scanner, many times I have been able to watch the effects of the mind on the physical body, and the way that energy travels around that body. For example, it's very easy to have someone stand in front of the video camera, and then observe the way energy travels around their body on the computer screen.

Likewise, it's equally simple for someone trained in healing to then affect the way energy moves around that person's body, simply using their mind, and to see these effects in real-time on the computer monitor. This can be done by focusing the mind with feeling on that person's body in a certain way, or by projecting energy (even from a great distance) to that person, and observing the effects.

In conclusion, our thoughts really do have a powerful effect on our environment, and especially on those around us. I do not believe it is an exaggeration to say that our thoughts have the ability to help or harm other people. And discovering this for yourself can be quite a shock, and it brings with it great responsibility for your actions in thought, word, and deed.

Please, don't just take my word for this. There are plenty of simple experiments you can try for yourself that can allow you to prove to yourself just how powerful your mind affects your physical body, your surroundings, and what happens to you, as you'll see in the next section.

But please be warned that should you use this knowledge and understanding to harm or hurt other people in any way, it will have even greater negative effects on your own life, making such stupid actions a very big mistake.

Do These Exercises: Two Simple Mind Over Matter Experiments

You really don't need a well-equipped laboratory to start doing experiments like Massaru Emoto or Harry Oldfield. This is because you probably already have in your kitchen everything you need to test several basic mind over matter experiments for yourself.

Experiment 1

This experiment is based on Masaru Emoto's similar experiment, that showed the effects of both positive and negative words and emotions on samples of cooked white rice.

This experiment is very easy to try, because all you need are three identical jam jars with lids, and some cooked white rice. You need to add around 4 heaped tablespoons of the rice to each jam jar. It's important to have approximately the same amount of rice in each jam jar.

Next, screw on the lid of each jar, making sure that each is sealed. Then label the three jam jars as A, B, and C. All 3 jam jars should be placed together in a room at normal room temperature for best results.

The next step is to focus your thoughts and emotions on jam jar A for about 10 seconds each day, projecting to it feelings of love, while saying the words "I love you".

Next, do exactly the same to jam jar B, but this time project feelings of anger, resentment, and hatred, or any other negative emotion you can imagine, while saying the words "I hate you".

Lastly, you need to completely ignore jam jar C, because this is your "control" sample to which you will compare the results of jam jars A and B.

If you do this correctly, and consistently each day in the manner I have described, after about one week you will start to notice that the rice in jar A is much clearer than the rice in jar B, which will be starting to become discoloured, or even mouldy. The control sample (jam jar C) will most likely also be discoloured, but not nearly to the same extent as jam jar B.

After continuing this experiment for 3 weeks you should see very big differences between jam jars A and B, with far more mould and discolouration forming on the rice in jam jar B. This simple experiment can show you the effects of your emotions on cooked rice samples.

You can also do this experiment using 3 plants, instead of cooked rice. Its best if you use young seedlings for this experiment, and keep the jam jars open.

By focussing positive thoughts and emotions on plant A, and by focussing negative thoughts and emotions on plant B, you can discover how quickly and vigorously plants grow in response to positive emotions and how negative emotions slow up and stunt their growth. You should notice a big difference in plants A and B in comparison to your control plant C, which is not focussed on at all.

See the process chart on the next page to clarify the exercise:

Experiment 2

There is another simple experiment that will give you even faster results. In fact, with this experiment you can almost immediately discovered the effects of your mind on physical matter.

You can see a demonstration of this mind over matter experiment in the second video of my free four-part video course "Change Your

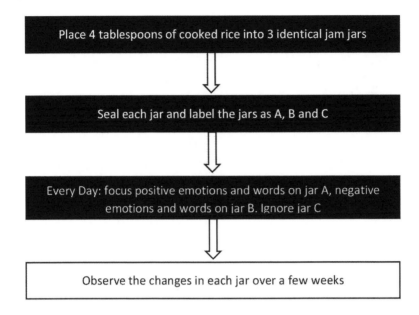

Thoughts Transform Your Life!", and you can get it here:

www.mikepettigrew.com/keys

For this experiment, you need some thick aluminium foil (the type you use when freezing food), a pin or needle, a ruler, a pencil, a pair of scissors and a pencil eraser (or a small lump of plasticine or modelling clay).

In this simple mind over matter experiment, you are going to create an energy spinner, and you can quickly learn how to make it spin clockwise, anticlockwise, and even get it to stop. You can do this, simply by focusing your mind and emotions in a certain way.

With a ruler or any straight edge, draw a cross shape onto the aluminium foil. Each leg of the cross should be approximately 1 inch (2.5 cm) long, and about a quarter of an inch (half a centimetre) wide.

With a pair of scissors, or a sharp knife you need to cut around the outline of the cross. Once you have cut out the cross, with the point of your pencil make a small indentation right at the centre of the cross.

Next, bend each leg of the cross at an approximate 45° angle. You now need to embed the base of the needle into the pencil eraser (or plasticine/modelling clay), which you will use as a base. The point of the needle should be pointing upwards, while the blunt end of the needle should be facing downwards. Finally, balance the aluminium cross on the tip of the pin. You have now completed creating your energy spinner.

By cupping your hands either side of the device (without actually touching it), and with a little practice, you should be able to quickly learn how to get the spinner rotating in both directions – clockwise and anticlockwise. The more relaxed you are while doing this, the faster the energy spinner will rotate. If you have any trouble at all getting the energy spinner to start moving, then bring up a feeling of gratitude. Gratitude can act as a powerful catalyst for affecting your physical body and your environment. It also allows energy to travel around your body more powerfully than before.

By focusing (or imagining) energy travelling down your right arm and out of your right hand, you should quickly be able to make the energy spinner rotate anticlockwise, faster and faster. Then, by focusing the feeling of gratitude down your left arm and out your left hand you should be able to make the energy spinner start rotating in the opposite direction.

It's quite easy to become proficient at this. And by focusing your mind and emotions in the way I have described, you can get the energy spinner rotating in either direction, and even make it stop spinning completely. However, it's important to not move the position of your hands while doing this experiment. Also, make sure your arms and hands are in a relaxed position and that they are not straining. The more relaxed your body and mind are, the better your results will be.

This is not about forcing something to move with your mind, as this can actually have the opposite effect. It is about having a "disinterested interest". In other words, intending the spinner to rotate, but not being concerned at all about whether it will or not. Feelings of gratitude and trust are enormously powerful, and these will make the spinner rotate far more quickly. Later we will discover how these same feelings can also be used in a powerful way to help you to achieve your goals.

See the process chart on the next page to clarify the exercise:

You Are What You Believe

Whether you are ready to accept it or not, your dominant thoughts, beliefs, and emotions draw into your life positive and negative

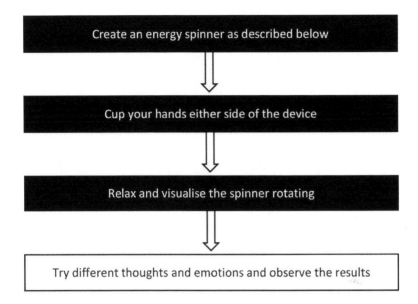

experiences. They really do determine what you can and cannot achieve during your life. And when you learn to control your inner life, you will have developed the ability to create anything you want.

Really, the only control you have in your life are the thoughts that you think, the beliefs that you hold, the emotions that you feel, the things that you visualise, and all the actions and reactions that you choose. In other words, whatever it is that you wish to change in your life can only be achieved when you control these things.

When you learn how to do this (and it's a lot easier than you may think), you will have the power to move your life in any direction that you wish, so you can achieve your life's biggest dreams.

Your thoughts, feelings, and beliefs determine the actions that you take at every moment of your life. Your actions in turn then determine the results that you experience. Therefore, what you think and believe has direct results on how quickly and easily you can achieve your goals. In addition, you have discovered how your thoughts and emotions can also affect your physical environment, even without you physically manipulating anything.

In the next chapter, we will look at how you can use your thoughts and feelings to create highly charged goals, so that you can achieve them in the fastest and most direct way possible.

Summary:

➤ **Your mind affects your environment** — Your thoughts and
beliefs affect your actions and achievements. However, they
may also affect your environment itself!

➤ **Energy cannot be destroyed** — Emotional energy can
influence your environment and other people. It can be used
as a powerful catalyst for change.

➤ **Your mind influences physical matter** — Thoughts and
emotions can affect scientific experiments, and influence the
outcome of those experiments.

➤ **Do your own experiments** — Prove to yourself that your
mind affects your environment, and discover the power to
create anything you want.

STEP 2: Create Highly-Charged Goals

Many people use goal setting systems that are completely devoid of emotion, yet emotion is a powerful catalyst for achieving your goals in the fastest, most direct way possible. How you feel about your goals determines everything, and the real magic happens when you set goals that truly excite you — goals that motivate you powerfully, and goals that really stretch your life.

When you find your Big Why for each of your biggest goals, as we looked at earlier, it gives those goals a lot more power, and it allows you to achieve them much more easily. Another reason why you drilled down to find the Big Why for your bigger goals is that it enabled you to see whether those goals were truly meaningful to you, or are just helping you avoid something you don't really want to face.

In this chapter, you'll learn how to **combine several goals that are closely related into a single, new condensed goal** – a goal that contains a <u>powerful motivating factor (PMF)</u>. A PMF is simply a type of goal that excites you greatly, and that you want to achieve very strongly.

You will also learn how to create a goal anchor (GA) that can add even greater emotional energy to your goals – so that your goals are *highly charged.* Highly-charged goals are truly unstoppable and can set in motion a chain of events that will help you reach your goals.

Emotionalising your goals with high energy is extremely important, and is one of the biggest secrets to achieving your goals a lot faster and far more effectively.

Do This Exercise: Condensing Your Goals

A PMF is similar to a Big Why in that it's all about uncovering and using strong emotion as a catalyst for achieving your goals. However, it's not quite the same thing. You drill down to uncover your Big Why *for your bigger goals,* whereas you can use a PMF *to empower every goal that you set.*

In this step, you'll combine the list of goals you created in your brainstorming sessions so you can **group together goals of a similar nature**, or goals that can help support each other. When you group these goals, you need to make sure that at least one of them is *extremely important* to you and that it contains a lot of desire or emotional charge—this is your PMF.

For example, <u>if you have a goal that is a deep desire to travel more</u> (this is your PMF), another goal to have more free time, and another goal to earn more money, in a job that you love, then you can easily group these goals together into one concise and much more powerful condensed goal.

Goals:
- ➤ *Travel more (your PMF)*
- ➤ Have more free time
- ➤ Make more money
- ➤ Work in a job that you love

Condensed Goal:
I will start working in a new job that I love, that will pay me more than [X amount] every month, and that will give me more free time, *so that I can travel as much as I want.*

In this example, we grouped together several related goals into a single condensed goal, with a PMF. Your PMF is the deep desire to travel more, and we have linked this strong desire to the other three goals.

When each of your condensed goals contain a PMF, it becomes far more powerful and energised. It becomes a highly charged goal, and just reading it can invoke feelings of excitement in you. This is exactly what we want – goals that truly excite you and that powerfully motivate you into action. Compare this to goals that do not contain a PMF – in comparison they can appear lifeless and dead.

At this point, you may start to realise that some parts of your condensed goals could be dependent on other parts of the condensed goals being achieved first, and you would be correct. However, it's possible to modify and reorder your goals later if you really feel that they not optimised correctly for your current priorities.

Also, it's possible that your priorities may change over time, and you could discover that you no longer feel so strongly about certain parts of your condensed goals. When this happens, you can adjust your direction and modify your condensed goals accordingly if needed.

However, you do need to be aware of a very definite danger whenever you consider changing your condensed goals. You need to be deeply honest with yourself and ask yourself — *do you really want to change direction, or do you want to change your goals simply because you are starting to doubt your ability to achieve them?* If this is the case, then you can counteract this limiting belief using the mind programming methods that I will share with you in step four. Changing your goals frequently is never a good idea, and it could slow down your progress greatly.

Here is a process chart to clarify the exercise:

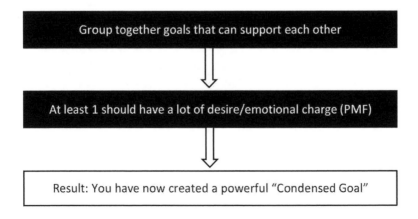

Possible Challenges: Setting Short-Term Goals

It's possible that you may have difficulty condensing some of your goals in exactly the way you would like right now, particularly if they are short-term goals that you wish to achieve within the next few months. With a short-term goal, it's often possible to condense it by **considering all the benefits** you will experience when you achieve it.

For example, if one of your short-term goals is to improve your relationship with your sister, as it has gone sour, then the benefits of achieving that goal are many. By healing the relationship, you and your sister will both be happier, and you will be able to share more good times together. Your sister's children and your own children will also be able to see each other more than before, and have more fun together. You may even be able to go on holidays together again, and confide in and support each other like you used to.

All these benefits from achieving your goal are actually goals in and of themselves – and could contain a PMF like this:

➤ *Heal relationship with sister (PMF)*
➤ Be more trusting - benefit
➤ Family have more fun together - benefit
➤ Go on holiday together - benefit

In this example, your condensed short-term goal could be written like this:

> *"By the end of next month, I will have greatly improved my relationship with my sister, so that she and I will regain our deep trust in each other, and so that we and our children can have holidays together, and have lots of fun together again."*

As you can see, even with short-term goals, it may be possible to create a condensed goal with a PMF by considering all the benefits you will gain by achieving that goal. When you do this, your short-term goals will be greatly energized and can be achieved a lot more easily.

The Power of Anchors

At the beginning of this book, I explained how I used my Crazy Gratitude Experiment to transform my circumstances. Within only a few hours of frequently bringing up the power of gratitude, I started to feel very differently and I started to see solutions to my problem that were not obvious to me before.

Then, once my dominant thoughts and emotions began to change dramatically, my environment started to reflect those changes in the form of synchronicities and opportunities that allowed me to completely transform my situation.

The way I did this was to "remember the feeling" of gratitude every 30 minutes of the day. At first, this took quite a lot of effort. However, there is an even simpler way of tapping into powerful positive emotions whenever you want. You can even do this automatically, and it's a method you can use to inject raw power into all your goals.

What I'm referring to here is a <u>Neuro Linguistic Programming (NLP)</u> technique known as anchoring. This technique is based on the famous experiment by Russian scientist Ivan Pavlov. Whenever Pavlov fed the dogs in his laboratory, he signalled the arrival of food with the ringing of a bell. After some time, he noticed that the dogs would start salivating as soon as the bell was rung, even if food was not delivered to them. The ringing of a bell was the anchor that triggered the dogs to get excited and start salivating at the prospect of food.

Do This Exercise: Create Your Own Goal Anchor

You can create your own anchor that will allow you to automatically experience any feeling you wish, whenever you want. All it takes is a specific touch, gesture, or word to trigger that anchor. It works just like a bookmark for a desired feeling, and you can recall it any time you want using the very same anchor.

This exercise will help you create your own <u>goal anchor (GA)</u> that you can use to greatly speed up the achievement of your goals. You will be using this simple yet powerful tool every day from now on to emotionalise and empower all your goals. Specifically, you will be using it every time you do your affirmations, and whenever you think about and visualise the achievement of your goals.

Step 1: Think about times in your past when you felt sincere deep gratitude, or a time when you felt truly happy and fulfilled, or a time when anything seemed possible to you. In terms of positive feelings, these would be "10 out of 10" experiences. Even though it may be difficult for some people to recall such experiences, everybody has had at least some experiences like this.

They could be experiences that you had as a child, as a teenager, or even later as an adult. They are times that you treasured greatly, where anything seemed possible. If you can recall experiences that also contained a lot of gratitude, then that's even better, because gratitude attracts more positive experiences into your life – especially when you bring up that feeling frequently.

Step 2: Next, write down a list of as many of these positive emotionally-charged experiences as you can possibly recall. Just write down a few words to describe each experience. For example, *"The time that I won a tennis match at school when I was 11 years old"*. If you can come up with ten of these "10 out of 10" experiences, that's ideal.

Step 3: Now, choose the top three experiences from your list that contain the most positive emotional energy, and cross off all the others.

Step 4: Recall each of these three experiences in detail, and engage fully with each memory – remembering the sights, sounds, smells, and feelings you experienced at that time. Really immerse yourself in the experience and relive it as vividly as you possibly can.

Step 5: Choose the experience that contains the greatest amount of gratitude, happiness, and positive emotions, and cross off the other two.

Step 6: Now, focus on that experience for a few minutes, again recalling it in even more detail than before. Engage fully with the memory and allow the feelings of gratitude, joy, fulfilment, or of anything being possible for you to build very strongly within you.

Step 7: At the point where you are overflowing with positive emotions — this is the exact moment you need to set your anchor. To set your anchor, simply touch the thumb and first finger of your right hand (or left hand, if you prefer) together and squeeze them together gently.

You can now trigger your GA whenever you are thinking about your goals. Just squeeze your thumb and first finger together to bring up those very same powerful feelings again. It really is that simple and it's extremely effective at bringing your goals to fruition! From now on, you will be using this anchor whenever you do your affirmations and whenever you are visualising your goals. Don't overlook this powerful tool.

No matter whether you are setting small goals, or life-changing long-term goals, this simple GA tool will be very important to you on your journey to success.

See process chart on the next page.

Baby Steps First

At this point, I do need to warn you. If you have experienced many setbacks during your life, and if you have become conditioned to expect failure, then it's important to get proof that this system works before you start setting really big goals for yourself.

Getting strong evidence that this system will work for you is crucial.

"Do you know who this is, Little Spike?"

Then once you start achieving small goals, you'll gain more confidence in your own ability, and you can go on to set bigger and bigger goals for yourself.

I'm not saying that you shouldn't set big goals from the outset. What I'm saying here is that any goals you set for the near future should stretch your life, but only by a little. You need to take baby steps before you can run. Self-confidence plays a huge part in achieving your goals, and you need to develop self-confidence early on in order to be able to achieve really big goals later.

The only thing separating you from achieving your goals right now is a certain degree of inner change, and this system will help you to bring about that change — in a gradual, consistent, reliable way. This goal achievement formula, along with the mind programming techniques you'll learn later, will work incredible magic in your life and allow you to start seeing results in just a few days.

Here is a process chart to clarify the exercise:

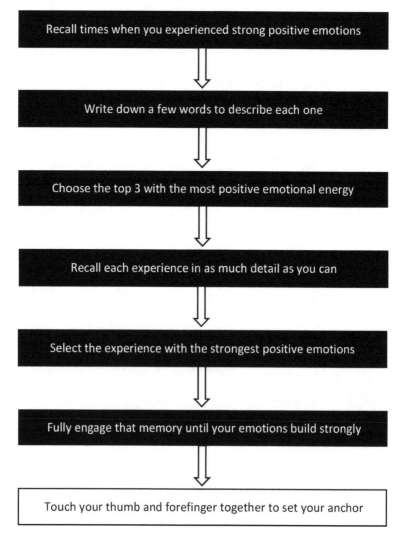

Summary:

➤ **Condense your list of goals** - Group them into goals of a similar nature, or goals that can support each other.

➤ **Identify goals that have a powerful motivating factor (PMF)** - Make sure that each condensed goal includes one.

➤ **Create your goal anchor (GA)** – Use it every day to inject strong emotional energy into your goals. This can greatly speed up the achievement of all your goals.

Your Subconscious Mind

Many scientists believe that our subconscious mind makes up 95% of our entire mind. Your subconscious mind is the part of you that is responsible for all the automated processes in your body. For example, you don't need to consciously will your heart to beat, or to force your lungs to breathe. If you did, then you would be in big trouble very quickly! All it would take to finish you off would be to fall asleep for a couple of minutes.

Fortunately, your subconscious mind is currently regulating and controlling all sorts of operations and processes in your physical body at this very moment, even though you are neither aware of it, or have conscious control over it. Now, I'm fully aware that you can use your conscious mind to slow down the beating of your heart, or to speed up your breathing rate. However, you really only have a very small amount of conscious control over most of what happens in your physical body.

Your subconscious mind is not just limited to controlling the automated processes in your body, but it is also responsible for all your successes and all your failures! This is because you carry within you all sorts of subconscious beliefs about what is possible and impossible for you. Sadly, those beliefs (that you may not even be consciously aware of) can sabotage all your efforts to achieve your goals.

Your Inner Navigator

Imagine you are on a ship travelling the ocean. However, the captain, who you had no reason to mistrust, starts changing direction, and he does this more and more as the days pass. As you gradually become aware of this, you become deeply shocked and realise that your captain is not to be trusted, and that you now have little chance of ever reaching your destination.

Now, imagine you are on a ship where you have a trustworthy captain who keeps moving in the direction of your destination — you can relax and enjoy the journey, absolutely knowing and trusting that you will reach it as quickly as the ship is capable of travelling.

Right now, your mind is probably a bit like the first captain, who keeps changing direction, and who never reaches his destination. Or, if he does eventually reach that destination, he takes lots of detours before finally arriving many months after the intended date.

Very few people take the time and commit to start using their mind in a way that gives exactly the results that they seek. As Shakyamuni Buddha said about 3,000 years ago, *"All is change, nothing is constant"*, and nowhere is this truer than when applied to the human mind.

How much control over your own mind do you currently possess? Can you say with absolute certainty that you have total control of your mind, your thoughts, and your emotions? Or do you find yourself frequently being blown off course by the events and changes in your circumstances?

These are very important questions, and if you can say yes to most of them, I can still assure you that most likely you have far less control over your mind and emotions than you may at first believe. You see, the part of your mind that is reading the pages of this book and thinking about what I'm saying is really only a tiny part of your mind!

In many ways, your subconscious mind is a bit like a giant supercomputer. It organises, processes, and stores in your memory your experiences, your thoughts, your words, and the action you make during your lifetime. Even if you consciously believe you can achieve something, but subconsciously you believe you are not worthy, not capable, not intelligent enough, or not confident enough to achieve it, then **your subconscious beliefs will always win out**.

Conditioning Determines What You Can Achieve

Your subconscious mind also determines your entire outlook on life. Many people make great efforts to achieve their life's biggest goals, but end up failing miserably, even though they seem to have done all the "right" things. In fact, when you set a big goal for yourself, and then go on to make a huge amount of efforts to achieve it, but end up failing miserably, it can have a very negative affect on your mind and your subconscious beliefs from that point forwards.

You can end up consciously disillusioned, and subconsciously believing that you just don't have what it takes to achieve your life's biggest dreams. These subconscious beliefs that have been formed through painful experiences can hold you back enormously.

The fact is, you have received all sorts of negative conditioning that is continually jeopardising your chances of achieving what you want from life. You have been conditioned from the moment you were born to think, act, and believe all sorts of things that are simply not true. You have been conditioned by your parents, teachers, friends, and peers, by advertising and what you see on TV, and especially by religions!

However, not much of the conditioning you have received is entirely accurate. I'm sorry to say that you have been lied to far more times that you can possibly imagine. And this is definitely not your fault, because when you hear the same thing again, and again, and again it always has an effect on you, whether you are consciously aware of it or not. We have all been brainwashed, lied to, kept small and powerless, and prevented from becoming what we are truly capable of.

It may seem that your subconscious mind (being the greater part of your mind) is actually your enemy, and that you have very little control over what it creates in your life, because it seems to sabotage every effort you make to succeed. It's easy to feel defeated and believe that there is little you can do to change the course of the tide. However, I'm delighted to say that you really can powerfully influence your subconscious mind, and overcome the conditioning that has held you back up until this moment.

One of the greatest secrets of the subconscious mind is that it can be influenced quite easily. After all, it is through repetition and through painful experiences that all your negative subconscious beliefs were created in the first place.

In the chapter after next, I will share powerful new techniques that will enable you to literally program your mind for success from this point forwards. These exciting new technologies have the power to totally rewrite the fabric of your destiny, and help you to achieve your goals faster than a speeding bullet, so you can become deeply happy, truly fulfilled, and live a life of greater meaning and purpose.

This is very exciting, because it means that you are no longer doomed to failure, and that your future is no longer determined by what has happened to you in the past. You really can recreate your life from this point forwards, and carve out a whole new chapter of experiences that will be both exciting and deeply rewarding. But first, in the next chapter let's look at the importance of adding a deadline to each of your goals.

Summary:

> **Your subconscious mind** — It makes up 95% of your mind, and it has a huge influence on all your successes and failures in life.

➤ **You have been conditioned** — You have been conditioned all of your life, and right now your conditioning is most likely sabotaging your goals.

➤ **You can overcome conditioning** — You can influence your subconscious mind and overcome your conditioning using powerful mind programming techniques.

STEP 3: Give Each Goal a Deadline

A fter creating your list of goals in step one, and then condensing them in step two, you should be left with a new shorter list of goals that will contain plenty of emotion — goals that you feel strongly connected to and that excite you.

As you have already discovered, strong motivation and excitement are very important factors in allowing you to achieve your goals, and have the effect of speeding up the achievement of those goals.

These strong feelings can also help you to overcome any temporary setbacks that you may experience while working towards your goals.

"I could swear the invitation said '7 am'."

Now it's time to regroup your condensed goals into long-term, medium-term, and short-term goals, and give each one a deadline.

Do This Exercise: Goal Regrouping

It is very important to **regroup your goals into realistic time frames.**
For example, if you set a very big life-changing goal that requires you to make lots of changes in your life, learn new things, and develop new skills, and that is also dependent on other goals being achieved first, it should definitely not be categorised as a short-term goal!

A short-term goal is any goal that you believe you can achieve within the next 3 months. It might require some effort to do so, but as I mentioned in step two, you need to be realistic and work within your current realm of possibility. As you become more experienced with this system, your confidence grows, and you start seeing it's benefits working for you, then you can start stretching your life more with bigger short-term goals.

Generally, when you start regrouping your goals into definite time periods, its best to start with your long-term goals first, and then work your way backwards to the present time. This way, you may start to discover new medium-term and short-term goals that you need to set in order to bring some of those long-term goals to fruition.

Long-Term Goals – The Next 5 to 10 Years

Write out a list of all the condensed goals you want to achieve in the next 5 to 10 years and beyond. Anywhere between 1 and 5 goals is perfect for this list, although if you want to add more, that's fine. You should include all your biggest goals in this list – those goals that may take a long time to achieve, and that may require other goals to be achieved first.

As you start achieving your medium-term and short-term goals more quickly, you may find that some of these long-term goals start to move on to your medium-term goals list. This happens when your ability to achieve your goals improves substantially, and you realise that you really can achieve any goal that you set for yourself.

Likewise, when your circumstances dramatically improve, you may find you can now easily achieve goals that you had previously categorized as long-term. By using this system consistently from now on, after some time will probably find yourself setting long-term and medium-term goals that may have seemed completely impossible to you just a few years back. These goals would never even have been on these lists, because you would have believed them impossible to achieve.

Medium-Term Goals - Within 1 Year

Next, create a second list. This is a list of all the condensed goals you would love to achieve in the next year. Again, anywhere between 1 and 5 goals will be fine. These are substantial goals that may take some time to achieve, and that may necessitate you learning new skills. However, they are not goals that should require a major lifestyle change to achieve.

Again, at the outset, you need to be more realistic than with your long-term goals, but as your confidence grows and you get proof that this system is highly effective, you may be able to move some of these goals on to your short-term goals list.

Short-Term Goals – The Next 3 Months

Finally, create a list of all the goals you would like to achieve in the next 3 months. Once again 1 to 5 goals should be fine. With this list, you need to be a lot more realistic. The goals on this list need to be achievable, although not necessarily very easy to achieve.

In this 3-month list, you should include goals that stretch yourself a bit. These should be goals that will show you clearly when you have achieved them that the principles in this system are valid and that they have worked for you. This will give you a lot more confidence, so you can go on to achieve your far bigger medium-term and long-term goals in the future. It's necessary to first take baby steps, get validation that the process works, and then go on to achieve even bigger goals having developed the confidence that the process works.

At this point, please ensure you **don't set crazy, unrealistic short-term goals** at the outset, like becoming a famous singer within the next 3 months! (Unless, of course, you already have great confidence in being able to achieve this, are already a highly talented singer, and have powerful media connections!)

By creating short-term goals that stretch your life too much at the beginning, you are only setting yourself up for unnecessary stress, failure, and great disappointment. Doing so could even have serious negative effects in that you may become disillusioned and start to doubt your own ability more than before you set such goals.

Set a Time Limit for Each Condensed Goal

With each condensed goal that you create, it's usually a good idea to decide on a specific date you wish to achieve it by. Now, I do realise that some of your long-term goals may seem very far off in the future and that it's hard to settle on a specific date for their achievement.

However, just by deciding on what appears to be a realistic date (by which you will have achieved a goal), can be very beneficial. It will have a powerful effect on your subconscious mind, commanding it to bring you the results that you seek — by that specific date. This is *because your subconscious mind needs very specific instructions* if it is to go to work on your behalf and bring you the results that you want.

When your subconscious mind has specifics to work with, it will start affecting your thoughts and feelings, and it will motivate you to take specific actions at specific times. These inner "promptings" will gradually steer you towards your goal — and within the timeframe you've set.

Your subconscious mind works in a similar way to a servo mechanism in a guided missile. First you need to set a target (or goal). Then, you need to launch that missile (by taking action), and set its arrival time (by setting a clear deadline). After this, the missile uses it's electronic "senses" to stay on target. This is known as "positive feedback".

When the missile starts to go off-target, it gets "negative feedback" and simply adjusts its course so it's back on track again. Likewise, sometimes it accelerates, while other times it slows down, all according to the deadline you have set for its arrival.

Your subconscious mind guides you towards your goals in a similar way when you give it the specifics that it needs to do its job. Just like the missile, the process that your subconscious mind takes to guide you to your goal is automatic. *So get setting!*

Here is a process chart to clarify the exercise:

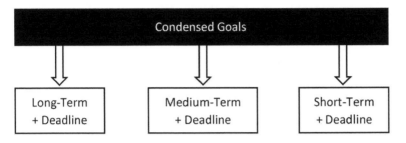

Here are some typical examples of deadlines (for goals set in July 2017):

Long-term goals:
> ➤ Goal 1 – deadline 31st December 2022
> ➤ Goal 3 – deadline 31st December 2025
> ➤ Goal 4 – deadline 31st December 2027

Medium-term goals:
> ➤ Goal 1 – deadline 31st December 2017
> ➤ Goal 3 – deadline 30th April 2018
> ➤ Goal 4 – deadline 31st July 2018

Short-term goals:
> ➤ Goal 1 – deadline 31st August 2017
> ➤ Goal 3 – deadline 30th September 2017
> ➤ Goal 4 – deadline 31st October 2017

Summary:
> ➤ Regroup your condensed goals – Regroup them into short-term, medium-term, and long-term goals.
> ➤ Include a deadline for each goal – This is so your subconscious mind has the specifics that it needs to bring you what you want.

Mind Programming Technologies

With every thought, word, and action you make during your life, you are either reinforcing deep set beliefs that you carry, or creating new beliefs. Fortunately, what you believe can be changed, and therefore what you experience can change too.

Our understanding of the brain, the mind, and human consciousness has evolved more in the last 10 years than it has in the entire history of the human race.

It is now possible to access all sorts of interesting and beneficial mind states using modern technology. You can achieve deeply immersive states, even if you are a complete beginner.

"There's something about our new team leader that is really energising"

In this chapter, I will share information with you about some of these exciting new technologies, so that you can experiment with them yourself and use them to enhance your life.

These technologies are used by millions of people around the world to attain consistent levels of high performance, and they are now within your grasp.

The Language of Your Subconscious Mind

If you have ever been disappointed because the efforts that you have made have not resulted in the changes that you wanted to see, then this chapter can help you enormously. The great news is that your subconscious mind is surprisingly easy to influence, and you can program your subconscious mind in any way that you need.

Your subconscious mind can be influenced powerfully through repetition and strong emotion. Whenever you repeat the same thoughts, especially if there are strong emotions present, then you are literally programming your subconscious mind according to those thoughts and feelings.

It really is possible to think your way into experiencing great loss in your life, just like I did. Likewise, it is equally possible to change your thinking and transform every area of your life in a very positive way.

Your subconscious mind is being influenced all of the time, whether you are consciously aware of it or not. Since this ongoing programming totally determines whether or not you can achieve your goals, doesn't it make sense that you learn how to influence it powerfully to bring you what you want? Learning how to program your mind for success is one of the greatest talents that you can ever learn during your life, because it will allow you to create whatever you want from this point forwards.

There are also several ways to uncover the self-limiting beliefs that have been holding you back, just as there are many ways to let go of those beliefs. Likewise, there are numerous ways to plant new programmes or beliefs in your mind that will help you to achieve your goals far more quickly than before.

You program your mind though repetition, and you can program it very powerfully when you add emotion to the process. Just like a child learning multiplication tables, all you need to do is repeat the same instruction again and again for it to influence your subconscious mind in a powerful way. It really is that simple!

When we repeat something again and

"It would take a miracle to motivate him."

again with emotion, we start to believe it. It's almost like the first time we say something, our subconscious mind doesn't take much notice. But after the third or fourth repetition, our subconscious mind starts focussing on the instructions we have given it, and it begins to take effect.

This is how brainwashing works, although that's making use of the subconscious mind in a rather negative way! It's also the reason why we see terrible crimes committed by religious fanatics who have literally been hypnotised into a way of thinking, believing, and acting.

Belief, or faith, is incredibly powerful, and it has the power to create miracles or terrible atrocities. And the way to create faith or belief in anything is through repetition with emotion. So, if you have a lot of self-doubt right now and you believe you are incapable of achieving some big goal, it's very possible for you to create a new belief that will counteract that negative influence.

The Power of Affirmations

One of the most common ways used by successful people to achieve their goals is to use the power of affirmations. Affirmations are simply positive empowering statements that you repeat to yourself aloud, both morning and evening, **with emotion.**

One of the most famous affirmations was created by Émile Coué; *"Every day, in every way, I'm getting better and better"*. Coué discovered the placebo effect, and he used this simple conscious autosuggestion to bring about transformation in his patients. In the next chapter, we'll explore in a lot more detail how you can create your own affirmations that will help you to transform any area of your life.

Affirmations are very powerful and they can help you to completely rewrite your internal programming, and erase all sorts of negative beliefs you may currently have — beliefs that are sabotaging your goals. You can also use affirmations to program your mind for confidence, happiness, empowerment, greater wealth, and success in any endeavour. They are simple to create, and equally easy to use.

The Benefits of Self-Hypnosis

Another way to powerfully influence your mind is to use hypnosis. I do realise that many people are afraid of hypnotism, as they have seen

"He decided to use hypnotherapy to confront his hatred of broccoli"

stage hypnotists who appear to take power over their subjects. These stage hypnotists seem to be able to force their subjects to do all sorts of embarrassing things that would normally be completely against their nature. However, there is a huge difference between stage hypnosis and autosuggestion, or **self-hypnosis**.

What's important to understand here is that with stage hypnosis, the hypnotist spends a lot of time finding the ideal subject. They usually invite several members of the audience to join them on stage, and one by one they eliminate those who are not "hypnotisable". The truth is, they choose a subject that they are certain will go along with the act. Someone who wants to take centre stage, and is not afraid to embarrass themselves.

In hypnosis, the subject always has control, and they can break their hypnotic state whenever they want. The hypnotist or hypnotherapist is not subjecting their will over anyone, and can never make their subject do anything that is against their nature. True hypnosis is simply a way of bringing your mind slowly and surely into a deeply relaxed state using guided imagery and suggestions.

The session usually starts with the hypnotherapist asking the subject to relax each area of their body in turn, often moving from the feet upwards. It is simply a very effective way of bringing your body and mind into a deeply relaxed state. A state where you are able to access your subconscious mind a lot more easily, and influence it with positive empowering statements.

However, it's not actually necessary for most people to visit a hypnotherapist to be able to benefit from hypnosis. Using a hypnosis recording can be extremely effective. There are thousands of self-hypnosis recordings available that you can buy to help you overcome all sorts of fears, create greater self-confidence, and improve virtually every area of your life.

Each self-hypnosis session starts with a relaxation induction, followed by a series of suggestions that will help you in very specific ways. The final part of each session slowly but surely brings you out of the hypnotic state to feel relaxed, recharged, energised, and fully alert.

Self-hypnosis is a deeply relaxing, refreshing, and empowering experience, and is hugely enjoyable. It can also quickly bring about great transformations in your life and how you feel on a daily basis. With hypnosis, it's even possible to overcome the effects of all sorts of negative experiences in your past, and in only a few sessions—experiences that could otherwise have taken years of psychotherapy to unravel.

You should investigate self-hypnosis yourself, and start using it to overcome any negative conditioning you are aware of. In step seven I will also share with you a way of uncovering this negative conditioning, so that you can root it out once and for all and stop it from holding your life back.

My program "The Millionaire Mind Secrets" has an optional upgrade that contains a *full success mindset programming toolkit,* that includes self-hypnosis recordings. Find out more at:

www.themillionairemindsecrets.com

Subliminal Technologies

Subliminal advertising has been banned in most countries because it's so effective at making people do specific things. This is where a word, a sentence, or an image flashes up on your TV screen so quickly that you are not consciously aware of it. However, your subconscious does notice it, particularly if it's repeated several times. The subliminal message then influences your thoughts, feelings, and desires.

This is a highly effective way of programming or influencing your subconscious mind. However, you can use subliminal messaging in a way that is constructive and helpful to your life, rather than having it influence you against your will.

There are several ways to use subliminal influences. There are many recordings available where specific positive suggestions are embedded in music, but are below the normal conscious hearing threshold. If you listen very carefully to such recordings, you can often hear "whispering" voices at various points in the music track.

Now obviously, you need to have normal hearing to make use of subliminal audio recordings, but they can be effective when played at sufficient volume, preferably through headphones or ear buds. Just like self-hypnosis, there are recordings available that can help you to overcome negative beliefs and disempowering thoughts, as well as programming all sorts of positive and beneficial new suggestions into your subconscious mind.

Some people mistakenly believe that technology and spirituality are at opposite ends of the spectrum, but this is simply not true. Technology has now advanced to the point where you can use it in powerful new ways to enhance your spiritual development, and your inner growth, and it can also help you to achieve your goals more quickly.

Program Your Mind While at Work!

If you spend a lot of time working at your computer each day, then there is an even more effective way of using subliminal messages to affect your subconscious mind.

There are computer programs available that will flash words and short statements onto your computer screen so quickly that you may not even consciously notice them. You can also vary the speed of the flashes so that nobody looking over your shoulder will notice them either! You can use these programs to flash all the affirmations you create onto your computer monitor thousands of times each day.

I have tested this technology myself quite thoroughly, and with great success. For example, last year, I increased the annual sales of one of my businesses by 70%, which was the exact amount that I had set to flash up on my computer screen many times each day.

Even though I took all sorts of practical actions to make this goal possible, I am certain that my subliminal program helped me to achieve this very substantial goal.

So, if you work in front of a computer for most of the day, it could be well worth investigating these programs and testing one of them for yourself.

The optional upgrade to the "The Millionaire Mind Secrets" program I mentioned on the previous page, also includes subliminal software and subliminal audio tracks.

Biofeedback

Biofeedback is a way of learning how to relax your body and mind deeply using a simple machine. The machine displays (or feeds back to you) your current level of relaxation. Often, this is in the form of LEDs on the machine itself, and a decreasing tone in the headphones connected to it. Quite quickly, you can learn how to switch off the LEDs one by one, and decrease the tones that you hear, simply by relaxing. The machine is controlled through electrodes that are placed on your skin, often on the palm of your hand. And as you relax, the resistivity (or the impediment to electrical current flow) of your skin reduces. And as your skin's resistivity becomes less and less, the LEDs blink out and the tone decreases.

After experimenting for some time using this machine, you can learn how to relax your body and mind in a truly profound way. Before long, you may not even need the machine anymore, because you will be able to enter a state of deep relaxation, just by using your mind, by remembering what that state felt like.

Back in 2001, an amazing game was created called "Journey to Wild Divine" and it was endorsed by people such as Dr Deepak Chopra and Dr Andrew Weil. The game was a biofeedback system that ran on an ordinary PC. Electrodes attached to the fingertips measured various changes in the body, including relaxation level.

The game was set in a virtual world that you needed to navigate, achieving lots of different goals along the way. In the game, you unlocked various different levels or experiences based on your ability to increase your energy, lower your heart rate, deepen your level of relaxation, as well as reaching other inner states.

Journey to Wild Divine was a "mind state training system", as well as a visual biofeedback system and it was a powerful way of gaining inner mastery — mastery over your mind and emotions. It was also very uplifting, and spiritual in nature.

Several other similar games were released, and I've also tested them, but in my experience, the original *Journey to Wild Divine* was truly exceptional, and one of the most profound and enjoyable biofeedback systems I have ever used.

The company has recently been acquired by Unyte and has updated its technology so that it can be used more effectively with modern devices.

For further details visit their website at: www.unyte.com

Brainwave Sensing Technology

At every moment of the day and night, your brain is producing all sorts of different frequencies or oscillations. On an EEG machine, this is visible as lots of peaks and troughs (or oscillations) in the readout. These are what are commonly known as brainwaves.

"Bernie, as soon as she's out zap her with the brain probe"

There are always certain frequencies that predominate depending on the activity we are doing. Scientists name the main brain states that we experience: alpha, beta, delta, and theta. For example, when you are wide awake and trying to figure out something, your predominant brainwave activity is in the beta range, which is approximately 15 - 18 Hz (or cycles per second).

On the other hand, when you are in a very relaxed but focused state, your brainwave activity is predominantly in the alpha range, which is approximately 7.5 - 12 Hz.

The theta state, which is approximately 4 - 7.5 Hz, is associated with deeply relaxed meditative states. It is also the doorway to your subconscious mind, where you can access forgotten memories, and is associated with accelerated learning and the dream state.

There have been many experiments conducted with yogis, psychics, and shamans, where it was found that when they are in their "psychic state", the brain predominantly produces these theta frequencies.

Finally, when you are in deep sleep, your brainwave activity slows down even further and the predominant frequencies are in the range 0.5 - 4Hz.

Up until quite recently, if you wanted to measure your brainwave activity, you had to spend an enormous amount of money on medical grade equipment. However, it's now possible to purchase low-cost devices that can pick up and display your brainwave activity using a mobile brainwave sensing headset.

These devices can be used with many fun brain-training apps to teach you how to meditate, relax, focus, and understand your mind better. Just like with other biofeedback devices, you can use brain-sensing technology to quickly learn how to control various events on the screen of your device, simply by using the power of your thoughts.

Like other biofeedback devices, you won't be using this technology to reprogram your mind directly, but it will enable you to bring yourself into a deeply relaxed and receptive state, where you can then program your subconscious mind very effectively.

When you gain more control over your own mind and your emotions, you will be able to start using it in miraculous new ways to improve your life. You can now learn how to meditate and experience all sorts of mind states that before would have taken many years to achieve, and you can do this easily thanks to the power of modern technology.

You can find out further information about brainwave sensing devices on these websites:

➤ www.neurosky.com

➤ www.choosemuse.com

Sounds That Create Expanded Awareness

For many years, scientists have been aware that repeated audible beats can have profound effects on a person's brainwave activity. For example, when you listen to a drumbeat, after a short time your brain waves start to mirror that drumbeat, and this is known as the frequency following response or FFR. This can easily be observed on an EEG machine.

Therefore, it makes perfect sense that if we beat a drum very slowly, for between one and four beats a second, it makes those who are listening to the drum feel very drowsy, and slowly but surely bring them into the sleep state. You can use sound to stimulate almost any brain state. For example, if you are finding it hard to focus, then by listening to frequencies that stimulate the alpha range, you can easily become more focused.

Millions of people around the world use sound technologies to improve their concentration, relax deeply, overcome insomnia, tap into the subconscious mind, and further enhance the effects of self-hypnosis. It is even possible to use regularly repeating rhythms such as isochronic tones, binaural beats, and monaural beats to enter deeply meditative states that were previously only available to those who had practised meditation for decades.

There are many recordings available today that can help you achieve all sorts of brain states that will enhance and improve your life. The great thing is that once you become proficient at reaching a specific brain state using sound, there comes a point where you may no longer need the method that originally brought you there.

The "Millionaire Mind Secrets" program also includes a collection of 24 binaural beat audio files you can use to explore this fascinating technology for yourself.

Light and Sound Machines

Sound is not the only method you can use to stimulate specific brain states. Flashing lights do exactly the same. For example, the flickering flames of a campfire can make you very relaxed and drowsy.

I experienced this phenomenon many times in my late teens and early 20s. I was studying electronic engineering at college, and every day I used to take the train between my home in Wicklow and the college in Dublin city. The journey took about an hour and a half each way, and during the summer months when the sun was shining, I discovered a very interesting phenomenon.

On days that were sunny, as the train rushed through the countryside, the flashing of the sun through the trees and bushes at the side of the railway track always made me very, very drowsy. Each time, before this would happen, I would be wide awake and studying my electronic engineering textbooks in preparation for my exams. But as soon as the train gathered speed and the flashing of the sun through the trees began, I would always become very sleepy.

The effect was so powerful, it almost forced me to fall asleep. I usually tried to fight it, but the drowsiness was often so overpowering that I could not resist it for more than a few minutes. Now it just so happens that the average speed of the train and the spacing between the bushes and trees made the repeating flashing of the sun fall into the delta range of brainwave frequencies that is associated with sleep.

On the other hand, when the train was speeding along far more quickly, the flashing of the sun through the trees made me much more alert and focused. Again, this is the frequency following response in action, but instead of using sound, in this case the stimulus was flashing light.

Now, consider for a moment what it would be like to combine both flashing lights and audible beats together. I'm sure you can imagine just how powerful the effects could be. There is exciting technology available today that can trigger any brain state you can imagine, and many that you cannot possibly imagine, simply by combining light and sound together. These amazing devices are called Light and Sound Machines, or Mind Machines and I have been experimenting with this technology since it came on to the market in the 1990s.

Several scientists and researchers are now even claiming that they could contribute significantly in the next evolutionary step for the human brain.

Researchers and scientists have even found that these devices can actually increase your intelligence, help you to overcome all sorts of bad habits and psychological conditions like ADHD, as well as improve your ability to master your mind and emotions. They even have the power to stimulate your long-term memory, allowing you to remember experiences in your past you had forgotten and improve your ability to focus and learn new information.

Most light and sound machines consist of a small box that's a bit bigger than a cell phone and they have at least two sockets. You plug a set of headphones into one socket, while you use the other socket to plug-in your light frames.

MindPlace Proteus budget Light and Sound Machine

The light frames are simply an ordinary pair of sunglasses, with a number of LEDs placed just behind the lenses. All you need to do is put on the headphones and the light frames, select a program, and close your eyes.

Many light and sound sessions are a visual feast. The patterns that you will see while your eyes are closed can be quite incredible. You will see all sorts of geometric patterns and shapes that are produced by the flashing LED lights, through your closed eyelids.

Warning: I should point out that people who are strongly affected by flashing lights should not use these devices. Those who suffer from photo sensitive epilepsy should never use a light and sound machine. They can use the headphones, but definitely not the light frames! However, for the vast majority of people, using these devices is very safe.

One of my very first experiences with one of these mind machines was very revealing. I decided to take a 30-minute break from my work, and try out the new light and sound machine that I had just bought. I tried a 30-minute relaxation session, because the day had been quite stressful, and I was very alert and wide awake before I started this session.

I lay down in a comfortable position, put on the headphones and light frames, and started the relaxation session. The patterns that I was seeing were stunning, and the tones coming through the headphones were very soothing. Very soon I started to relax deeply, in fact a lot more deeply than I expected! Suddenly, my phone started ringing, and I awoke from the middle of an amazing dream. To my complete astonishment, only 10 minutes had passed since I had started that light and sound session.

As you can imagine, I was totally shocked and amazed by the powerful relaxation effect after only 10 minutes. I certainly didn't intend to fall asleep — that was the last thing I wanted to happen! So, the next time I decided to do a light and sound session during the working day, I made sure it was a short session and it was not called "Deep Relaxation"!

I have had many remarkable experiences while using this exciting new technology, and I now own several mind machines. With some of these devices, you keep your eyes open while looking out on what appears to be a white featureless void, that then transforms into swirling colour patterns. These open-eyed devices seem to be more suited to achieving states of peak performance, accelerated learning, and improved focus.

On the other hand, most devices use light frames that you use with your eyes closed and these seem to work best with relaxation and inner exploration type sessions. Either way, you can still expect great results no matter which type of light frames you end up using, and some machines allow you to use both types.

When you combine a light and sound session (particularly when you choose the right type of session) with self-hypnosis, the effects can be incredibly powerful. Of all the modern technologies that are now available to help you influence and change your subconscious mind, I find these mind machines truly remarkable.

You can find out more about the latest light and sound machines, and how to use them on the following websites:

> www.mindplace.com
> www.photosonix.com
> www.neurotronics.eu
> www.amazon.com
> www.mindmachines.com
> www.toolsforwellness.com

Creative Visualisation

There is another very powerful way to influence your subconscious mind to give you what you want. Creative visualisation is where you visualise clearly what it is that you want. It's a type of consciously focused daydreaming, where you focus on the outcome that you wish to experience.

"Visualise yourself not falling off the wall"

You simply think about what it will be like when you have achieved your goal. Try to imagine exactly what will happen when you have achieved your goal. Really try to feel what it will be like. Try to imagine what you will see, hear, feel, and experience once you have achieved your goal. By really trying to imagine the feelings, and by making those feelings build up into excitement, and deep gratitude, you are taking a very powerful step towards achieving the goals you are visualising.

Your subconscious mind doesn't know the difference between what you want and what you don't want. Your subconscious mind simply goes to act on your dominant thoughts and emotions, no matter what they may be. So, if you are constantly obsessing about what's wrong in your life, or deeply fearing what might happen, then these are passed to your subconscious mind and influence it deeply.

It's even possible to create the very things that you dread in life simply because you repeated these fears with emotion again and again. I have experienced this myself, and definitely would not recommend it! This is an example of using creative visualisation in a very negative way, and I believe we are all guilty of doing this to varying levels, at some point in our lives.

On the other hand, when we fantasise about how wonderful it will be when we have achieved our goal, and start injecting excitement and gratitude into our visualisation, then our subconscious mind goes to work in every way that it can to help us to achieve that goal.

It's probably a very good thing that what we visualise takes time to manifest. If our subconscious mind manifested all our desires instantly, then we would all be in pretty big trouble! Can you imagine what it would be like for someone who is petrified of dying in a plane crash to actually take a flight? If our subconscious mind acted instantly on our worst fears, then our world would be in a far worse state than it is in right now.

So, when you take time to really think about and visualise the excitement and gratitude you will feel when you have achieved your goal, it can dramatically speed up the achievement of that goal. And the more you can imagine all the wonderful ways that it will affect your life once you have achieved that goal, the better.

We have all been told by teachers that daydreamers never achieve much in life. However, this is simply not true. In fact, a study at University of California, Santa Barbara, found that people who let their minds wander were 41% better in creative thinking tests than other people. Also, many of the world's most successful people were daydreamers. These include such famous scientists as Albert Einstein and Isaac Newton.

By continually focusing on something wonderful, that excites you, and that you have a deep burning desire for, you are empowering your subconscious mind to bring you what you want. Now, rest assured, I'm not saying that our kids should spend their time idling away their hours while at school. However, I am saying that you can use consciously controlled creative visualisation to powerfully influence your subconscious mind to bring you what you want. And in step four you will start using this wonderful tool to speed up the achievement of all your goals.

It's almost like your subconscious mind is Aladdin's genie, that goes out and does your bidding, and rather than only getting three wishes, you get unlimited wishes that can bring you whatever you want. You really do have this amazing resource within you that is far more powerful than you can possibly imagine. And when you start connecting with your subconscious mind using the technologies I have described, and start influencing it in as many ways as you can, you will be able to speed up the process of achieving your goals by at least 10 times.

Summary:

➤ **You are responsible for your beliefs** — Your thoughts, words, and actions determine your beliefs. By changing your beliefs, you can change your experiences.

➤ **Language of the subconscious** — Your subconscious mind is influenced by repetition and strong emotion. You can use these to change your internal programming.

➤ **The power of affirmations** — Affirmations are a simple, effective way to program your mind, so you can achieve your goals more quickly.

➤ **Benefits of hypnosis** – This is a simple, safe, and effective way used by scores of highly successful people to overcome their conditioning and achieve their goals more quickly.

➤ **Subliminal technologies** – This is an effective way to influence your subconscious mind, so you can program it more efficiently, using subliminal voices and images.

➤ **Biofeedback** – This is a simple way to relax your body and mind so deeply that you reach the hypnotic state easily, so you can reprogram your subconscious mind for success.

➤ **Brainwave technologies** – There are powerful new ways to bring yourself into a deeply relaxed, focussed state where you can embed new programs into your mind.

➤ **Creative visualisation** — This is a highly effective way to embed positive, empowering images into your mind of what it will be like when you have achieved your goals.

STEP 4: Program Your Mind

One of the most important steps in achieving any worthwhile goal is to **program your mind so that your success becomes almost automatic.** You need to make impressions on your subconscious mind so that it constantly steers your life in the direction you want to go, while at the same time overcoming any internal blocks that may be holding you back.

One of the most effective ways of programming your mind is to use affirmations. Every thought that you think and every word that you say is an affirmation. Your internal dialogue is literally a continuous flow of affirmations and this has a dramatic impact on your life! Whatever you repeatedly say and think (especially when strong emotions are present) creates your beliefs and your life experience at every moment.

Bill didn't always pick the best places to program his mind

Many of your beliefs may simply be learned thought patterns that you have developed since childhood. Some of these beliefs may work well for you, while others may be working against you.

If not changed, negative thoughts and negative beliefs can be very destructive. They can literally sabotage every chance you have of achieving your goals. In this chapter, you will learn how to create powerful affirmations that program your mind for success. And affirmations that can help you overcome negative thoughts and beliefs, as well as several tools that can enhance your results.

Program Your Inner Supercomputer

The more you repeat something with emotion, the more powerfully it will affect your subconscious mind. The great news is that it's possible to program your mind using affirmations to help you to achieve your goals, instead of experiencing continual sabotage.

When you manage to do this successfully, your subconscious mind will constantly be on the lookout for opportunities that you would normally not even notice. These opportunities can bring you much closer to achieving your goal.

You may experience these opportunities as synchronicities or coincidences that appear almost like magic. It may even appear like some higher power is now working on your behalf, which really is true because your subconscious mind is unlimited in what it can do for you. Your subconscious mind is what connects you to universal wisdom, and it is more powerful than any supercomputer ever created. It can literally work miracles in every area of your life and help you to achieve anything you truly desire.

However, you must know how to use it correctly for it to bring you the results you desire. Unless you are speaking the same language as your subconscious mind, all your efforts could be in vain. This is because your subconscious mind has its own unique language, and you need to be able to use at least a small part of that language if you are to succeed in getting it to do exactly what you want.

A part of the language that your subconscious mind understands is **repetition**, as well as **strong emotion**. Your subconscious mind is also strongly influenced through **visualising** what you want.

When you repeatedly visualise what you want and inject strong desire into those visualisations, the supercomputer of your subconscious mind will help you create virtually anything you could ever wish for in life.

So, you are now going to create another simple yet powerful tool that you can use to influence your subconscious mind to consistently create what you want.

The Power of Affirmations

To create this tool, you need to rewrite each of your short-term, medium-term, and long-term goals as affirmations. These affirmations will powerfully influence your subconscious mind to bring you exactly what you want. The type of affirmations you will be creating are simply **positive empowering statements** that you say to yourself aloud.

For the very best results, you should read your affirmations aloud while triggering your GA, when you wake up in the morning, and again last thing at night before going to sleep. Whenever you read your affirmations, you should always trigger the goal anchor (GA) that you created in step two. Your GA will add strong positive emotions to each of your affirmations, which will affect your subconscious mind very powerfullAffirmations can also be designed to help you to re-program your thought patterns so that any harmful underlying beliefs can be replaced with more potent positive beliefs about yourself and your capabilities.

Affirmations are one of the most effective methods you can use to powerfully influence your subconscious mind, and they are very easy to create and use. For an affirmation to be really effective, you need to create it correctly.

Your affirmations need to:

➤ Be personal – using the word "I"
➤ Be in the present tense – "I am", as though your goal has *already* been achieved
➤ Be positive
➤ Be specific – this may include a time reference
➤ Include at least one dynamic emotion or "feeling" word such as "grateful"
➤ Include an action word (ending with "ing") such as "learning", "enjoying", or "growing"
➤ Not too wordy – *clear, concise, and easy to remember!*

Example Affirmation:

Say for instance one of your goals is to find a more fulfilling job where your talents are used more fully and where you are rewarded by your future employer with a much higher wage than you are currently receiving. You might construct an affirmation like the following:

"I am grateful for my deeply fulfilling job as [state the type of job you want], which is paying me [state the amount you want] every week."

If your goal needs to be achieved by a specific date, then add a definite deadline to it. For example, "By March 30th 2019" or "Before my 35th Birthday" etc. So your affirmation would be:

"I am grateful for my deeply fulfilling job as [STATE THE JOB YOU WANT], that I begin by [STATE DATE YOU WANT TO START], and which is paying me [STATE AMOUNT YOU WANT] every week."

Do This Exercise: Convert Your Condensed Goals into Affirmations

Now it's time to convert all your short-term, medium-term, and long-term goals into powerful affirmations that program your mind to help you achieve those goals. You need to rewrite each one of them using the method I have just described.

Let's take, for example, our condensed goal that we created in step two of this system - in the chapter named "Create Highly Charged Goals".

Goals:

➤ *Travel more – powerful motivating factor (PMF)*
➤ Have more free time
➤ Make more money
➤ Work in a job that you love

Condensed Goal:

I will start working in a new job that I love, that will pay me more than [X amount] every month, and that will give me more free time, *so that I can travel as much as I want.*

We can easily **convert this condensed goal into an affirmation** that will program our mind to achieve it more easily, like this: *"I am making [X amount] every month, working in a job that I love, having lots of time to travel to all the places I want."*

Or if you want to achieve this goal by a specific date (which is advisable), the affirmation could read like this: "By [DATE] I am making

[X amount] every month, working in a job that I love, having lots of time to travel wherever I want"

Of course, in this example, it's far better if you know exactly what type of job that you want (for example, Senior Marketing Manager) and name it specifically in your affirmation! It's important to be as specific as you possibly can when creating your affirmations – your subconscious mind needs those specifics to work with, so you can get the very best results.

At the back of this book, I have included an affirmation library that you can refer to. It will help you get inspiration to create your own affirmations. However, please don't shortcut this very important exercise by just using the affirmations from the library — it's vitally important that you **create your own unique affirmations based on your own condensed goals.**

Here is a process chart to clarify the exercise:

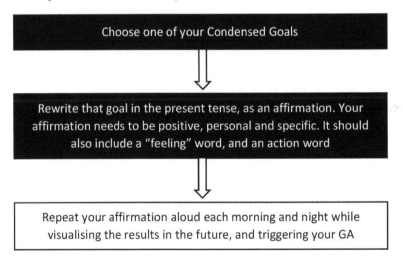

Affirmations Can Overcome Negative Thoughts

It's also very valuable to create affirmations that counteract negative self-limiting thoughts and beliefs that you currently hold about life, yourself, and your capabilities.

For example, if you have a rather pessimistic outlook on life, and if you often feel low on energy, then you might consider repeating the following affirmation aloud and with emotion several times each day: *"Today, I am full of energy and overflowing with joy."*

Even though right now you may be feeling the complete opposite, **providing you do this affirmation regularly while triggering your GA**, you will start to feel its powerful effects on your daily outlook and energy levels.

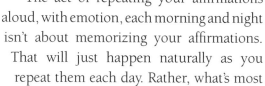

On the other hand, if you have the tendency to blame others instead of taking 100% responsibility for your life and all that happens to you, then you might use an affirmation like this: *"I am the designer of my own life and I take full responsibility for creating my own success and happiness"*

If you often feel like you are a failure, an affirmation like this could help: *"I possess all the qualities that I need to be very successful."*

The act of repeating your affirmations aloud, with emotion, each morning and night isn't about memorizing your affirmations. That will just happen naturally as you repeat them each day. Rather, what's most

He tried to be positive no matter the atmosphere

important here is that when you repeat your affirmations aloud each day, you need to remember to *visualise* and *emotionalise* your affirmations for them to be most effective.

You need to imagine them as though you have already achieved your goal. The more strongly you work up feelings of achievement and deep gratitude, the more powerful the effects will be. Triggering your GA will help you greatly in bringing up these positive feelings.

Affirmations really are a simple yet wonderful stimulus for change in your life. With affirmations, you can program your mind for success, and rewrite the negative conditioning that has been holding you back for so long. They also have the power to transform your beliefs about yourself and what you can achieve.

In addition, affirmations can weaken negative impulses, change what you focus on, and improve your perceptions. They can transform your desires, improve your emotions, and dramatically speed up the achievement of all your goals.

Combining Affirmations with Technology

In the last chapter, I shared with you several powerful new ways you can use to program your mind for success. Technologies that can help you achieve your goals more easily. These methods included light and sound machines, subliminal technology, bio feedback devices, and hypnosis.

You can use your affirmations with any of these methods for even greater effect. This is because, when you reach a deeply relaxed, focused state, your subconscious mind will be most receptive to any instructions you give it, and these technologies can help you greatly.

For example, if you spend a lot of time in front of a computer, it would be well worth installing subliminal software that you can use while you work. You can add your own affirmations to this software, and have those affirmations flash up on your computer monitor so quickly they are impossible to read with your conscious mind.

Using subliminal software is not a replacement for repeating your affirmations aloud morning and evening, but it is a powerful way to make lots of additional impressions on your subconscious mind. This in turn, can greatly speed up the achievement of your goals.

Using Creative Visualisation

As well as reading your affirmations aloud while triggering your GA, each day it's also important to visualise the sort of things that you will be experiencing when you have achieved these goals.

Really feel the sense of joy, fulfilment, empowerment and gratitude that you will experience when you have achieved them. To do this effectively, it could help to ask yourself this question: *How will I know when I have achieved this goal?* When you achieve your goal, there will be plenty of things that will show this to you. You will feel a certain way, and you will see very specific changes in your life.

For example, if one of your goals is to make a lot of money in your business, then when you achieve that goal, you would see this very clearly in your environment and lifestyle. For example, whenever you look at your bank statement, it will show an excitingly high balance.

You might also visualise yourself travelling the world, basking in the sun, hearing the waves lapping on the shore, and how great it feels to have the time and freedom to do whatever you want.

Work yourself into a state where you can almost reach out and touch these experiences as though they were happening to you right now. The more clearly you can use all your senses and emotions to do this, the better. This is where you can use your GA that you created in step two to charge each of your visualisations with powerful emotional energy.

Daydreaming when done in this way can be highly effective, and it is known as creative visualisation. Creative visualisation can dramatically speed up the achievement of your goals.

Some people believe that they are not able to visualise things clearly in their mind. However, I believe that it's impossible to live in this world without the ability to visualise what we are going to do next. If we were unable to visualise anything, then we would be unable to do anything! This is because before we take any action in our life, we first visualise that action. Even the act of getting out of your chair requires your ability to visualise at least to some degree.

For many people, what they visualise in their mind may not be very clear, and that's perfectly okay. There are very few people who have the ability to visualise with great clarity. Even if you find it difficult to visualise in your mind's eye, just do as best as you can.

Try the following exercise to get an idea of the power of creative visualisation to affect your own physical body.

Do This Exercise: Creative Visualisation

Imagine there is a big juicy orange in front of you. Now, imagine yourself picking up that orange and smelling it. Feel the weight of the orange in your hand and the texture of the peel. Is it warm to the touch or is it cool? Run your fingers over the peel and feel all the little pores on its surface. What colour is the orange? Is it a light orange colour or a dark orange?

Now, with your thumb, break into that orange. Smell the zest of the orange and imagine some of the juice flowing over your fingers. Imagine slowly peeling off all the skin of the orange, and breaking it in half. Next, imagine breaking off a section of the orange and putting it in your mouth. If you are like most people, at this point your mouth will probably start watering. This is just some of the power that your mind has over your physical body.

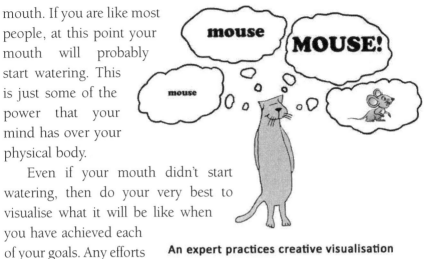

An expert practices creative visualisation

Even if your mouth didn't start watering, then do your very best to visualise what it will be like when you have achieved each of your goals. Any efforts you make to visualise while repeating your affirmations will be richly rewarded.

When you are doing your affirmations like this, it may appear that you are just tricking yourself into seeing and feeling something that is not based on your current reality at all, and in a way, this would be correct. However, it's important to remember here that by doing this, you are speaking the language that your subconscious mind understands, and you are commanding it to create the things that you deeply desire.Compare this to feeling negative and pessimistic about your life and your future. If you choose to do that, then you will truly reap what you sow through your thoughts and your feelings.

The fact is that affirmations together with creative visualisation work very effectively. By stating your affirmations properly like this every day, it can have dramatic effects on your future, and even how you feel in the present. The more impressions you make on your subconscious mind, the quicker visible results will materialize for you.

Create a Vision Board

If you have already defined your goals and how you want your life to be, then it's time to illustrate them visually. It's easy to create an inspirational collage of images that represents the image of your future. This acts as a tangible example, idea, or representation of where you're going in life.

Many people use vision boards to help them improve their ability to visualise the future they want. Vision boards are simply a board where you paste a collage of images.

These are images or representations of the things you wish to create in your life.

The saying "A picture is worth a thousand words" is certainly true. You can use any images that inspire you, and you can find them in magazines or on the internet. Representing your goals and your ideal life with pictures, images, and text can help to stimulate your emotions and enhance your ability to visualise the future that you want to create.

Your subconscious mind will also respond strongly, because the images you present to it, together with your emotions, create the vibrational energy that is responsible for manifesting your desires.

For example, if one of your goals is to buy a new house, then you could add images of your ideal home. Or if you want to be so successful in your career that you are interviewed on TV, then you could paste images of a famous TV presenter with your own image right next to them — so it looks like they are interviewing you on TV.

Once you have created your vision board, look at the images on it each day and you'll find that its effects on your subconscious mind can be considerable. You may find that it helps you feel even more excited about your future and your goals. This may sound very simplistic, and it is – but it's also very effective.

Create a Mind Movie

There's also software available that you can use to create a mini "mind movie" including your affirmations. These mini movies can bring together all sorts of images (both static and moving) with music, and you can combine these with your affirmations as text.

You can then watch these mind movies for a few minutes each day and they can have a similar, and possibly more powerful effect, than using a vision board. You can find out more details about mind movies at www.mindmovies.com

Your subconscious mind is powerfully influenced by the images that you present to it, so vision boards and mind movies can certainly be of great benefit to you.

Summary:

> **Convert your goals into affirmations** – Convert each of your short-term, medium-term, and long-term goals into an affirmation.

> **Repeat each affirmation morning and evening** – Read them aloud while triggering your GA, and visualise what you will experience as though you had already achieved it.

> **Create a vision board or a mind movie** – This can make even more positive impressions on your subconscious mind.

> **Use mind programming technologies** – For example, try light and sound machines, subliminal software, biofeedback, and hypnosis to complement and enhance the effects of your affirmations.

Magnifier: Positive Mental Attitude

O ur outlook on life determines everything. If we have a pessimistic outlook, then this attitude will affect our thoughts, our emotions, and all our actions. This in turn will determine the results we experience.

No person is wholly positive or negative — we are all a combination of both. There are times when we feel positive and enthusiastic, and where everything seems possible. Likewise, there are times when we feel deeply unhappy, and powerless to change our circumstances.

If you have received a lot of negative conditioning from an early age, as well as a barrage of painful experiences during your life, then your outlook on life will generally reflect this. When you have had a difficult life, it's easy to become cynical, yet this could mean that achieving your goals will be difficult, unless you do something about it that is.

For the most part, if we allow ourselves to remain disillusioned and cynical about life, then it will be very difficult to change our circumstances, and achieve our dreams. Of course, it's not possible to go from being deeply negative to instantly becoming a positive thinker. However, it is possible to slowly and gradually change your outlook and how you view what happens to you — and as you change your self-image, you can start to achieve what was impossible for you before.

Self-Image

Many years ago, Dr Maxwell Maltz, author of the bestseller *Psycho-Cybernetics,* discovered how people's self-image can be responsible for their successes or failures in life. Dr Maltz was one of the early pioneers of cosmetic surgery, and he treated many people who had become disfigured during accidents. He noticed a very interesting phenomenon.

After "waving the magic wand" of his scalpel, he found that many of his patients went through incredibly positive transformation in their personalities, becoming confident, outgoing, and successful. Such was the effect of restoring people's beauty, or at the very least transforming their disfigurement into normal appearance.

While he found that many people's entire lives were transformed through his cosmetic surgery, there were some people whose lives did not change at all. He found that in some cases, after having restored a person's physical beauty, there was no change at all in their personality or how they lived their lives.

Maltz discovered how important a person's self-image is to how they progress through life and develop. For example, if a person believes they are still scarred within, or that they are worthless, or lack intelligence, or are not capable, then this determines everything. As human beings, how we view ourselves determines who we are at every moment, and what we can become.

You Can Control Your Mind

The only true control you have in your life is your ability to control your mind and your ability to choose how you react to changing circumstances. Most people like to complain and moan about things from time to time. But if we find ourselves begrudging life, feeling disillusioned most of the time, or tend to blame our circumstances on other people, then this is something we need to address if we wish our life to change in any significant way.

Having the tendency to point the finger and blame other people for our misfortunes is very damaging on every level. When you view the world through the lens of blame, it may appear that everybody is against you, that you are a victim, and that you yourself are being blamed. However, this is usually not the case, and it's just

"I certainly hope you have some new complaints because mine are all the same."

the result of your perceptions.

One of my mentors once said something to the effect, *"The difference between our mind of complaint and our mind of appreciation may appear quite subtle. But, over the course of time just like particles of sand accumulate to form great mountains - whichever we allow to dominate, will have a huge effect on how our life turns out".*

If you are currently a negative thinker, then it is simply not possible to achieve very big goals until you change your self-image, and your attitude to life. Fortunately, this is easier than you may believe. At the beginning of this book, I shared with you how I changed my own negative thoughts and beliefs at a time in my life where I had experienced great loss. I had become pessimistic and disillusioned, and it seemed like I had lost all my self-confidence. However, by practising my Crazy Gratitude Experiment everything started to change.

This is because gratitude acts like a giant magnet, drawing into your life what you need to achieve your goals and to create a truly happy, creative life. On the other hand, resentment and complaint can destroy all your chances of becoming truly happy, and these feelings can even repel opportunities to achieve your goals in life.

Give and You Will Receive

There is a New Age concept known as the law of attraction, and people who try to use this law in their lives often believe that just projecting positive thoughts and emotions is enough, and that this is all they need to attract everything they want from life.

They believe that if they just ask the universe for what they want, then providing they continue to project thoughts and feelings that are positive, then they will get exactly what they want. Sadly, they are very mistaken — the universe does not bargain in this way.

While our dominant thoughts and emotions do have a very big effect on what we can and cannot achieve in life, the saying "Ask and you will receive" is totally incorrect. Rather, it's far more accurate to say "Give and you will receive".

When we make efforts to contribute to the lives of others, then it is us who benefit the most. And the more efforts we make to contribute to society, then the more opportunities we will attract into our own life. On the other hand, if we feel that life has given us a raw deal and that life owes us something, then we will inevitably be disappointed. When we are negative for a long period of time, it even pushes away all sorts of possibilities that could have happened to us.

Just like particles of sand accumulate to form great mountain ranges, over time the "particles of negativity" that you allow to build up can form massive impediments to your happiness and the possibility of achieving your goals. It's just not possible to attract great good fortune into your life when you are full of resentment and complaint. Even if you are only internally critical, it will still have some effect on what you can achieve.

We are all human, and we all have a mixture of positive and negative, light and dark, resentment and appreciation. However, what we allowed to dominate in the long term really will determine how our life turns out.

Choose Happiness Now!

Most people believe that happiness is something we feel *after* achieving something. Or that they are happy when their life *turns out* a certain way. However, research has found that happiness is not a result, but rather it is a cause that we can make.

Our universe is made up of causes and effects. Everything that happens is an effect of causes that have been made in the past. And as human beings, we make causes all the time in thought, word, and deed. If you believe you can only be happy when something wonderful happens to you, then you are mistaken, and you are only postponing the possibility of happiness right now.

Happiness really is a choice. You choose at every moment how you react to your circumstances and how you wish to feel.

As Dr Maxwell Maltz said, *"Man is by nature a goal-striving being. And because man is "built that way" he is*

not happy unless he is functioning as he was made to function – as a goal-striver. Thus, true success and true happiness not only go together but each enhances the other."

Dr Maltz is saying that success and happiness always enhance each other. And when life is difficult, providing you are still taking actions to achieve your goals, it's still possible to be happy.

Happiness is actually a state of mind that you choose, just like any emotion that you experience. We may believe that our happiness or sadness is created by external factors, but it is not – it is within us all of the time, but it is often triggered by external stimuli.

When we choose to create a strong, enduring happiness in our life, then as external factors change, that state of happiness is not so easily swayed. On the other hand, when we constantly blame our circumstances or misfortunes for not allowing us to be happy, then we are not taking full responsibility for our life. The universal law of cause and effect states that everything that happens to us is a result of our own actions and reactions.

Now I do realise that many people are born into very difficult circumstances, and that opportunity has a large part to play in what we may become. Also, many people experience painful and traumatic experiences that can lead to low self-esteem and other limiting beliefs. However, when you examine the lives of highly successful people —

people who have transformed society — in many cases, they have come from backgrounds of great poverty and all sorts of limitations.

Remember, our immediate circumstances never define who we are and what we can become. We have an amazing resource within us that enables us to achieve whatever we want, providing we think in the right way and take the right actions.

You Have the Power to Change

As you've seen, the human brain is more powerful than any computer ever created, and it is connected to unlimited wisdom that can be tapped into when needed. You have within you right now all the resources you need to surmount any problem, change any situation, and become capable of achieving everything you want. Never allow your present circumstances or complaint to define who you are and what you become.

I'm not saying here that you should start living a lie, and should just try to convince yourself that you are already happy and successful. What I am saying is that you have within you the ability to change your inner state whenever you choose to do so. You have the capacity within you to choose your dominant thoughts and emotions, and you have a choice at every moment of your life.

Whenever you feel stuck emotionally and you want to move out of that state quickly, just try triggering your GA. This will immediately unlock the negative loop of thoughts and feelings by triggering these new powerful positive feelings. This immediately breaks the loop – it is not suppression, rather it is you choosing how you wish to feel. This ability to shift your thoughts and emotion whenever you want is very simple, yet deeply empowering.

Human beings have an amazing capacity and capability to choose how they think and how they feel. Many people get very upset when something bad happens, or when they have an argument with a loved one, and this upset can often last days, or even weeks. Now, it's not wise to suppress any emotion, but we do have great ability to let go of strong negative emotions once they have fulfilled their purpose. Likewise, we also have the choice of holding onto such feelings, for as long as we wish. When we do this, we only hurt and punish ourselves in a very unhealthy way.

No matter what situation you experience in life, you can choose what you wish to do with it. You can either focus on what's wrong, and how you are a victim, or you can gradually move your focus towards resolving the situation.

It's really a matter of becoming solution-focused, rather than problem-focused. It's very easy to look at a problem and consider all the difficulties that it will create for you. However, when you start focusing on solutions to the problem, everything can change a lot more quickly for you. When you focus on problems, you become disempowered, and you cut yourself off from the wisdom that resides within you.

On the other hand, when you start focusing on solutions, then your mind kicks into a much higher gear and you feel empowered, even though the situation may not change immediately. Which you choose has an immediate effect on how you feel right away and the creative abilities you can tap into. Why put off experiencing happiness to a later time, when you can experience it right now – simply by choosing it?

Do This Exercise: Become Solution-focused

Here is an exercise you can do that will help you to move from being problem-focused to solution-focussed whenever you are facing a big obstacle in your path.

STEP 1: Write down the name of the problem you are currently facing. For example, "The problem with my boss".

STEP 2: Next, write out up to 10 ways this problem is causing you to suffer.

STEP 3: Now, write out at least 10 things that you are learning about yourself from this situation.

Step 4: Finally, write out at least 10 positive things that could happen once you have overcome this problem.

Here is a process chart to clarify the exercise:

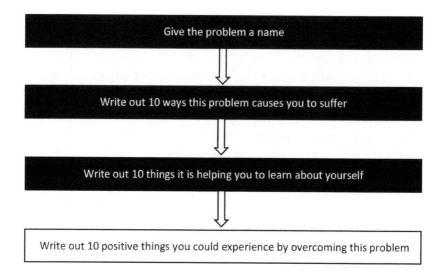

This simple exercise will help you to think in creative new ways, and it can also help empower you to change the problem. For example, you may discover that the current situation, though unpleasant, is giving you several opportunities to grow as a person and possibly develop new skills you didn't have before. It may even have the potential to open exciting new doors for you.

Creating a Positive Mental Attitude

You can create your own positive mental attitude through consciously choosing to do so, as well as by using the mind programming technologies at I shared with you earlier in this book, such as affirmations, hypnosis, and subliminal programs.

If you want more happiness in your life, you need to choose to feel it now, instead of waiting for something "good" to happen in the future.

Although it's better to create your own affirmations, here are a few examples you can test for yourself to choose happiness:

> ➤ I create my own happiness, and I choose to be happy now.
> ➤ I am happy and grateful for my life.
> ➤ I am grateful for all the wonderful things I already have in my life.

> ➤ I focus on all that is positive.
> ➤ I am in control of my thoughts.
> ➤ I am in control of my life.

You Can Transform Any Situation

Even though happiness is a choice that we make, when we are suffering, we often focus a great deal on ourselves and the problem we are experiencing. Unfortunately, when we are constantly focusing on our own problems, we can end up cutting ourselves off from all the wisdom that is available to us.

When life is very painful and we cannot find a way forwards, it's a bit like being in a dark room with the door closed. We can't see anything around us. But imagine for a moment there is a brilliant white light on the other side of that door. Right now, the door is closed so you cannot see your way forwards. But imagine what happens when you open the door by just a crack. Even though the door has hardly been opened, the light floods in and you can start to see everything in the room, as it becomes illuminated by the light.

When you are experiencing great suffering and you cannot see your own way forwards, it is possible to illuminate your situation and start discovering all sorts of solutions that were not obvious to you before. Gratitude has this power, and by testing my Crazy Gratitude Experiment for yourself, you can start to see your way forwards again and kick-start your inner creativity.

You have within you amazing resources, but when you are suffering deeply, it's almost like you cut yourself off from all that wisdom. But all you need to do is open the door just a crack to find a powerful new way forwards. When you change your emotions, even if only a little, then you can unstick yourself and find solutions that were not available to you before.

How to Deepen and Strengthen Your Happiness

Another powerful way to magnify your happiness, particularly when you are suffering greatly, is to contribute more to those around you. When you are suffering, that is the very time you need to make more efforts to help other people who are also suffering.

Often, when we are suffering greatly, we can end up cutting ourselves off from others, or even isolating ourselves, but that is not what

"That's not what your father meant when he said I had a heart of gold."

helps us most.

When we try to encourage others, even though we are suffering ourselves, it allows us to tap into great inner wisdom that was not available to us before. It is another wonderful way to light up that dark room.

The act of focusing on the happiness of others, who are also suffering, gives you immediate temporary relief from your own problems, and it can also connect you to creativity and wisdom that can help that person.

There have been times in my own life when I have suffered greatly, and when I just wanted to isolate myself from everyone. But I discovered that by trying to encourage friends who were also going through a rough time, it immediately transformed my own suffering and I always started to feel very differently myself.

Even though my own situation had not yet changed at all, I found that the more I encouraged and inspired others at such times, the happier and more confident I myself became.

When you make the effort to help someone who is suffering, it always has the effect of reducing your own burden and pain to some extent.

I have even found myself encouraging my friends by sharing analogies with them that I had never even heard before! This can often happen when you go out of your way to help another person who is suffering greatly — as you encourage them, you can tap into deep wisdom that lies within you, and that can help them overcome their problem.

To create long-term, deep, sustained happiness, you need to develop a more outward-looking attitude and help others to the best of your ability. Likewise, whenever you are trying to achieve a big goal, you can do so a lot more easily when you know that others will benefit from it too.

Going the Extra Mile

Many years ago, Napoleon Hill taught us the importance of going the extra mile: *"The importance of rendering of more and better service than that for which one is paid, and giving it in a positive mental attitude."*

Whether you are self-employed or work for someone else, going the extra mile means that you make a little more effort than most people ever do – or by showing more thoughtfulness than others. When you start developing this habit, other people will begin to take notice of your additional efforts. But that's not all – through cause and effect, whenever you make greater efforts, you also receive greater effects.

For example, if you are in business and you consistently overdeliver to your clients, giving them a better service that they expected, or showing them how much you value them as clients, then they will appreciate you far more than you may possibly imagine, and it will also deepen their trust in you.

In effect, it will make you stand out from all the rest. Businesses that always go the extra mile are the ones that thrive and grow and the ones that everybody ends up raving about. By always going the extra mile, your life or businesses can become a truly massive success.

Now, it would be easy to mistakenly believe that I am talking about self-sacrifice here, but I am not. Just by making a bit more effort than before, or by showing your gratitude, or that you care — you will be richly rewarded. The truth is, most people never go that extra mile and therefore they never get to understand the benefits of doing so. In fact, if you continue doing what most people do, you will always get what most people get — and sadly that's just a dissatisfying mediocrity.

On the other hand, by developing the habit of frequently asking yourself how you can give more to those people who rely on you, you will create big changes in your own life, in your environment, and in your circumstances.

As you develop real care for the people who you're helping, and give them more than they expect, then it attracts all sorts of beneficial coincidences into your life. When you start acting as a powerful catalyst in the lives of the people whom you're serving, then life always supports you even more in return.

Napoleon Hill explains the importance of developing the habit of going the extra mile as follows:

> *"The advantages of the habit of going the extra mile are definite and understandable. Let me examine some of them and be convinced. The habit brings the individual to the favourable attention of those who can and will provide opportunities for self-advancement. It tends to make one indispensable, in many different human relationships and it therefore enables him to command more than average compensation for personal services. It leads to mental growth and to physical skill and perfection in many forms of endeavour thereby adding to one's earning capacity. It protects one against the loss of employment, when scarce and places him in a position to command the choicest jobs.*
>
> *It enables one to profit by the law of contrast since the majority of people do not practice the habit. It leads to the development of a positive, pleasing mental attitude, which is essential for enduring success. It tends to develop a keen, alert imagination because it is a habit which inspires one continuously to seek new and better ways of rendering service. It develops the important quality of personal initiative. It develops the self-reliance and courage. It serves to build the confidence of others in one's integrity. It aids the mastery of the destructive habit of procrastination. It develops definiteness of purpose, insuring one against the common habit of aimlessness.*
>
> *There is still another great reason for following the habit of going the extra mile. It gives one the only logical reason for asking for increased compensation."*

By going the extra mile, you show others your appreciation, care, and gratitude. This may be a lot easier to put into practice than you may think, yet the effects on your relationships can be enormous. It will make you visibly stand out in front of the people whom you are serving.

Here is a thought-provoking saying that illustrates this: *"There are no traffic jams on the extra mile"*. This is because almost nobody goes the extra mile, so it's easy to take advantage of this fact. Going the extra mile makes you stand out clearly in comparison to other people, and is really a gift that you give to yourself, because of the benefits that it can bring into your life.

Do This Exercise: How to Go the Extra Mile

Step 1: Write out a list of the people in your life (or customer if you have a business) who you help in some way on a regular basis.

Step 2: Now, write out at least 10 ways that you could show greater appreciation to those people. Or if you have a business, you could also write out 10 ways that you could give added value to your customers.

Step 3: Finally, choose one that is not difficult to put into practice, but that clearly shows your appreciation, and how much you value those people or customers. Again, this is not about self-sacrifice! By giving a little more to others, you are really giving a lot more to yourself.

Here is a process chart to clarify the exercise:

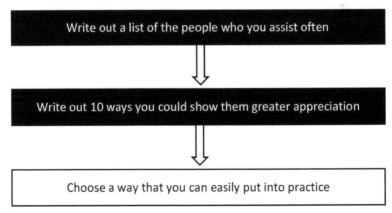

Treasure Yourself

There is also another way to enhance your happiness and well-being. It's important to treasure and appreciate yourself, no matter how many mistakes you have made in the past. It's so easy to blame ourselves

You are a masterpiece

and feel guilty for all sorts of things we have done in the past.

Many people belittle themselves all of the time, and this is really sad, because they are unaware of just how much this affects their life. This can happen because of experiencing many failures, and hardship during life, as well as deep ongoing conditioning. However, if allowed to perpetuate, these attitudes can have a devastating effect on all areas of a person's life.

Feelings of self-loathing, worthlessness, guilt, and blame can completely destroy lives. The only way to counteract such beliefs is through self-appreciating actions and powerful mind reprogramming.

Hypnosis, affirmations, and the other technologies I have shared with you will be enormously helpful here.

Also, when you reward yourself whenever you make any progress towards your goals, this can help to overcome such negative beliefs.

Taking the time to treasure yourself is important, and very worthwhile. Some people treat themselves to a new experience every week, and this can also help a lot in learning to treasure our own life.

How we feel about ourselves, determines how we feel about others, and ultimately what happens to us.

Summary:

➤ **Develop a positive mental attitude** – It's the key to happiness, and will bring all sorts of wonderful opportunities to you.

➤ **Improve your self-image** – It is responsible for all your successes and failures in life. Improve it and you can achieve your goals a lot more easily.

➤ **You can control your mind** - It's the only real control you have in your life. Therefore, when you control your mind, you can control your life.

- ➤ **You can be deeply happy** - Happiness is a choice. When you treasure yourself, and develop a more caring attitude, you also deepen your own happiness.
- ➤ **You have the power to change** - By becoming solution-focused, you can overcome any problem and change any situation more easily.
- ➤ **Going the extra mile** - By showing appreciation and by making a bit more effort, you stand out from the crowd and reach all your goals more quickly.

STEP 5: Plan for Accelerated Success

Many people who set goals fail to achieve them, simply because they have not planned their journey to success. Not planning properly is a bit like not having clear goals – either way, you can end up drifting through life and just reacting to changing events in your environment. If you don't make plans for the achievement of your goals, then you will just be relying on luck, and you will have no guarantee of achieving them - unless of course they are very small goals.

The fact is, **you simply cannot achieve any substantial goal without making adequate plans**.

As the saying goes "failing to plan is planning to fail", and that's why thorough planning is the next critically important step in achieving your goals.

The Procrastination World Championships were only a month away, He never trained so hard.

Do This Exercise: Create an Action Plan for Each Goal
In this step, you'll create your <u>action plan</u> – a list of the action steps that will help you to move towards each of your goals. You need to write out all of the action steps you can possibly think of that will help you reach each of those goals.

Even though you may not know exactly what all these steps are right now, it's still very important to start by writing down all of the steps you can currently think of. Later, you can add more action steps as they become more obvious to you.

Here is a process chart to clarify the exercise:

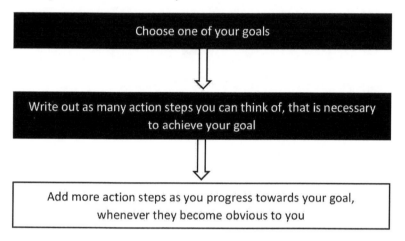

So, you need to begin by examining each of your goals and figuring out the steps you need to take to bring them to fruition. For example, if you're planning to start a new career as a writer, there are several steps you need to include as part of your plan.

Partial Action Plan for Becoming a Successful Author

➤ To become a skilled writer — do a course on creative writing
➤ To find the best writing style for your genre — read top bestsellers in that genre
➤ To be a successful writer — study how successful authors achieved their success
➤ To write your book – write for 2 hours each day, eliminating interruptions
➤ To get your book published – find out what publishers want for a successful book

Each of your action steps are really mini-goals in and of themselves. Some of them may need to be carried out in a specific order, while others may be implemented alongside others. You can decide yourself what's best in your particular circumstances and in what you are setting out to achieve.

Achieving worthwhile and meaningful goals entails plenty of careful planning like this. When you do this planning, and pay attention to the small details like I have just described, you can be assured of achieving each of your goals far more quickly than if you hadn't taken the time to plan adequately.

At this point, if you're still not sure what all those action steps need to be, then don't worry. Just by making a list of some of the initial steps that you can think of, it will benefit you enormously. When you start writing things down, it's amazing how quickly your mind starts to organise itself. You will find new ideas you had previously not thought of, as they start to become obvious to you.

In any creative exercise like this, **just getting started** is what truly matters. This kicks your mind into higher gear and it will start presenting you with new thoughts, ideas, and actions you would probably never even have imagined. In other words, the process of planning will itself help you to think more creatively.

Then, later as your plans start to progress, you can fill in the blanks by adding any new action steps you may need. On the other hand, if you ignore this very important step in achieving your goals, then your results could be disappointing.

The ancient Chinese philosopher Lao-Tzu once said: "A journey of 1000 miles begins with a single step". You now need to take an important step yourself by creating an action plan for each of your goals, and then you need to take another step by putting those plans into motion.

These really are some of your biggest steps yet, because they make the difference between just hoping you might reach your goals and *actually making it happen.* Very few people do this, and it's a huge reason for their failure to achieve their goals.

Mind Mapping

There's a wonderful tool that will help you brainstorm the action steps you need to take to achieve your goals, and it's called mind mapping.

Mind mapping is a way of getting your thoughts and ideas out on paper, and it can help you to think both logically and creatively to come up with new ideas you might never have even considered.

Mind mapping helps you to literally "map out" your ideas and gain greater insight into the plan you are creating. It stimulates your brain to think in creative new ways, and it can be a very exciting process. Your results may even surprise you.

You may find that after only a short time creating your mind map, you can figure out far more of the action steps you need to take than you had ever believed possible. Mind mapping mirrors the way your brain actually works, and this is why it's such a powerful brainstorming and planning tool.

When you create a mind map, you are converting a list of possibly monotonous information into a colourful, memorable, and highly organized map or diagram that works perfectly in line with your brain's natural way of working.

The great thing about creating a mind map is that you can put your ideas down in any order — as soon as they pop into your head. Then later, you can easily reorder them and move them about in the map to a place that makes more sense to you.

When you are creating your own mind maps, always start with a central idea — the goal you want to achieve. You then branch out from that goal to all the steps or actions you currently believe that you need to take to bring it to fruition. The branches leading out from your central idea represent the key thoughts in your thinking process, while the secondary branches represent your secondary thoughts about those key thoughts, and so on.

Example of a Mind Map

Here is a sample mind map for creating a healthier lifestyle that I created in about 10 minutes using iMindmap Ultimate. This excellent mind mapping tool was created by Tony Buzan, the inventor of mind mapping.

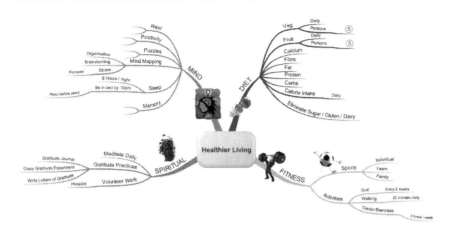

There are also many other mind mapping programs available today for both PC and Mac, and mobile devices, and many of them are free.

Here is a list of some mind mapping programs you might like to try for yourself:

➤ Bubbl.us
➤ Coggle
➤ iMindMap
➤ MindMeister
➤ MindManager
➤ MindNode
➤ Mindomo
➤ SpiderScribe
➤ Stormboard
➤ XMind

Create a Mind Map for Each of Your Goals

Now you know the importance of mind mapping and how helpful it can be in discovering your own action steps for each of your goals. So, from now on, you should start creating mind maps for all your goals. You will find that this process is not only great fun, it's also a powerful way of discovering what you need to do to achieve each of your goals.

Begin by creating a mind map for one of your short-term goals. You can create it on a sheet of paper, or using a software program (most are very easy to use). Once you have completed your first mind map, you will see for yourself just what a wonderful tool you have at your disposal.

I've been creating my own mind maps for many years and using them to plan every book, speech, lecture, and training program I create. I'm confident that you'll also find the ideas start flowing out of you easier than ever before. It's an exciting and very empowering process!

From time to time, as you progress towards each of your goals, remember to revisit its mind map to discover any new steps you need to take. A mind map is often in a constant state of flux, as new ideas pop into your mind. That's why it can be a good idea to have one on your phone that you can modify anytime a new idea comes into your mind – add it to your mind map before the idea disappears!

Focusing Questions

Creating your action plan is extremely important, but how can you really know which actions will bring you the very best results? After all, you only get 24 hours each day, so it's always best to focus most of your efforts on the things that make the biggest difference.

The Pareto Principle (or the 80/20 rule) says that 20% of the things you do get 80% of your results. It's a helpful rule to apply to almost anything you do, because it can help you focus on the things that really matter the most.

When looking for ways to implement this, it's great to examine how experts in the field operate. Brendon Burchard is a highly influential thought leader, and whenever he wants to create anything new, he does research to discern what will really matter the most on his journey to achieving it.

He then asks himself 5 important focusing questions:
> What moves the needle most?
> Where does the greatest long-term impact come from?
> What are the time wasters?
> What is a lot of activity but gets no real progress?
> "Where should I focus?"

For example, if you want to promote a new business that you have just launched, there are many ways you could consider doing this. Some could be easy to implement but give very little impact, while others may be more difficult but could be of long-term benefit to you.

To find out the best course of action you can take, these focusing questions can be enormously helpful. Whenever you ask yourself these questions, you may find that you might have to spend a lot of time on some possibilities, but get very little return on your time investment.

Others may take up very little of your time, but could cost a lot, like running a magazine advertisement. This also may only give you a very short-term boost in sales, whereas a low-cost social media advertising campaign may gradually get you a lot more customers in the long term.

This is just one example, and the answers to these questions will depend on all the factors and possibilities that are currently available to you.

The One Thing

In the Wall Street Journal bestseller *The One Thing*, Gary Keller and Jay Papasan reveal a similar technique in the form of a single question that you can ask yourself. This question can help you to focus on what's truly most important at any moment, whenever you're trying to achieve anything in your life.

That question is: *What's the ONE thing I can do that by doing it, everything else will be easier or unnecessary?* This is a focusing question that will **force** you to find the most effective way to achieve any action step, while eliminating distraction and anything that is not truly essential. It's a question you can ask yourself every day, for everything you are trying to achieve at work, in your personal life, and when working towards your goals.

For example, if you want to get more media exposure for your book, company, or brand, then you could phrase your question like this: *What's the ONE thing I can do to get maximum exposure for my book [or company/brand], that by doing it, everything else will be easier or unnecessary?*

Some years ago, I asked myself this very question to get more publicity for my new book *Unlock Gratitude Now! – Your 7 Keys to a Happier and More Successful Life*. There were all sorts of possibilities available to me. I could have focused on advertising, social media, press releases, radio and TV interviews, joint ventures with other authors, and other possible strategies. It made me look at all the different possibilities that were available to me, and to look even deeper to see what might be involved in each method of promotion.

By asking myself this focusing question, it forced me to narrow down my options to only those that would give me the biggest effects for the minimum amount of effort – those methods that would truly be the most efficient and effective.

Bridge to the Future

After asking myself this question, I decided to contact radio and TV stations by email. It worked out very well, resulting in lots of interviews in only a short period of time. This in turn gave my book exactly the exposure it needed, bringing it to bestseller status in Amazon within only a couple of weeks.

It only took a few hours work to get all these interviews lined up. Compare this to the days (or even weeks) of work it could have entailed had I used other marketing and advertising methods, which would probably have resulted in far inferior results, and at a much higher cost.

Since only 20% of the things you do generally bring you 80% of your results, the ONE thing focusing question in combination with Brendon Burchard's five focusing questions will help you sift through all the possibilities available to you, so you can eliminate the actions that are not the best use of your time and energy.

This can help you enormously in creating the most powerful action plan possible for each for your goals, and it will ensure you are always taking the most efficient and effective actions you can possibly think of.

Consistent Daily Actions

It's also vitally important to your success that you **take consistent daily actions towards each of your goals, even if it's only a tiny step.** Small consistent daily actions over time mount up to truly massive results in your life, because they act as a bridge to the future you want to create.

Many people start a great plan, but few continue when they encounter the very first hurdle, such as a temporary setback that rocks their self-confidence. This is really sad, so commit to yourself right now that **you will never be one of those people who try and then just give up at the first setback.**

The fact that you are reading this book is very encouraging, and you should congratulate yourself. It shows that you want to be a winner in life, and that you're looking for a better way to achieve your goals – a way that really works. Put each of the steps in this system to work in your own life and I promise that your life will never be the same again.

Remember, you need to take consistent daily actions in a way that gives you the maximum results possible from the minimum amount of effort.

Even if you take only a single small step each day, over the course of one year, this can add up to a lot of progress towards achieving your life's biggest goals. On the other hand, if you don't take consistent daily actions, then your results could be disappointing.

You may feel that your life is already far too busy to start taking meaningful daily actions towards your goals, and this is completely understandable. However, in Step 6 "Be a High Performer", you'll learn powerful high performance techniques that will help you free up your time, get a lot more done each day, and progress all your goals more quickly.

These high performance techniques can help you improve your focus, boost your energy, and greatly reduce your stress. This way, what may have appeared difficult before becomes a lot easier to implement — without you experiencing overwhelm or burnout. But first, in the next chapter let's look at the importance of optimising your health, and how this can also have a big impact on speeding up the achievement of your goals.

Summary:

> **Create your action plans** — Action steps help you to move towards each of your goals. Use mind mapping to stimulate creativity and see your path more clearly.

> **Use focusing questions and the 80/20 rule** – This will ensure that you always take the most effective, efficient actions that you can possibly think of.

➤ **Add more actions steps** – As they become obvious to you, add more action steps.

➤ **Take action every day** – Take daily actions so you make consistent progress towards your goals and see the results of all your efforts.

Magnifier: Health and Wellbeing

Science tells us that our body and mind are deeply interlinked, and how we think and feel directly affects our body and how it functions. Strong negative thoughts and feelings can even trigger the brain to release harmful chemicals into the bloodstream. As a result, we can literally poison ourselves through our thoughts and emotions.

Likewise, it has been found that positive thoughts and emotions help support and strengthen the body's functions.

"Tell me this isn't celery."

However, this mind-body relationship also works in reverse. Whatever food we feed our body with, will also have a profound effect on our mind, emotions, physical stamina, and energy.

Therefore, any program on accelerated goal achievement would not be complete if it did not also include this very important fact.

Increasing Your Brain Power

If you want to achieve big goals, but you are not looking after your body, eating nutritious food, or doing sufficient exercise, then this could be slowing down your progress in many areas of your life.

Now, I'm certainly not a health freak, but I do know from my own personal experiences that I feel quite differently and have a lot more energy and vitality when I am getting adequate exercise, drinking plenty of water, and eating high-quality natural foods. These things give me a lot more power and clarity of mind, and have played a big part in enabling me to achieve my goals more easily.

Whenever I eat badly for a few days, for example when I'm travelling, I notice that I become more sluggish, my thinking is less clear, and I get distracted more easily as my focus is reduced. Science also backs this up, therefore it is important for you to pay more attention to the food that you eat, the exercise that you do, and ensure that you drink plenty of water each day.

Water is so important to your body and mind — only when you are drinking sufficient water can the nutrients in your foods be carried to the cells of your body, so that those nutrients are used fully to power and repair your body.

Also, if you don't drink enough water, toxins build up in those cells and they can't be carried away and excreted by your body. These days, a huge number of people are suffering from chronic dehydration, so much so that their thirst mechanism no longer works properly — and dehydration can cause all sorts of chronic conditions.

Health Body – Healthy Mind

How much water you drink each day is obviously important, but so is what you eat. Are you eating foods that give you high energy, life-force, and a crystal-clear ability to think, or are you poisoning your body with all sorts of food and drinks that sap your energy and make you feel groggy and sluggish?

Only you can answer this, but it's something to consider deeply if you are serious about achieving big goals in your life. If you want to become highly successful and achieve everything you truly yearn for in life, then it's important that you seriously consider gradually improving your overall energy and vitality, and clarity of mind in every way that you can.

"How was Pilates?"

136

Your brain is more powerful than any supercomputer ever built, and just like a supercomputer, it will only operate effectively when you give it what it needs – a sufficiently clean power source and an environment in which it can operate effectively. When you improve your diet, drink adequate water to hydrate your body, eliminate toxins, get adequate exercise, and have sufficient sleep each night, everything will become easier for you — and you will have a renewed energy and enthusiasm for life.

Why is it that most health programs and diets never seem to focus on the most important organ in our body? The organ that regulates and controls every part of you, and also how you think and feel?

Yes, your brain has needs too, and if they are not addressed, then nothing else in your body will work nearly as efficiently. Nutritious food, plenty of water, exercise, and sufficient sleep will give you far greater clarity of mind and enable you to think faster and more effectively.

When you give every organ in your body (especially your brain) what it needs, you will be richly rewarded. Not only will you have more energy and be more efficient, but you'll experience dramatic effects in all areas of your life, what you can achieve, and how happy you can become.

In the early part of the twentieth century, Edgar Cayce summed up the components for maintaining a healthy life in the acronym C.A.R.E.

C: Circulation…we can only become healthy when our circulatory system is functioning correctly. Without proper circulation, the body's ability to heal itself is severely impaired. The natural healing processes of the body are increased by helping the circulation of blood around the body through exercise. Therefore, we must get sufficient exercise each day.

A: Assimilation…. Assimilation is the body's ability to digest and distribute food efficiently. For our body to assimilate food properly, we need to be eating high-quality natural foods instead of foods that have been highly processed.

R: Relaxation…. Relaxation includes not only getting enough sleep, but also setting aside time for recreation. It is vital that we get sufficient relaxation as well as sleep, so that we can restore both our mind and our body.

E: Elimination…Unless our body is successfully getting rid of the waste and toxins that build up in it, we can experience all sorts of long-term and chronic problems. When your body is not getting rid of toxins effectively, then it can affect your health, your energy level, your clarity of mind, and also your mood.

"Actually, I'm porridge intolerant."

To become a high performer and thereby achieve all your goals as quickly and easily as possible, it would be very beneficial for you to **make a lifestyle choice right now**. All it takes is a decision – a decision to live more fully from now on, by taking better care of the needs of your body and mind. <u>By doing this, you will be giving yourself the greatest gift possible</u>. A gift that will bring you more energy, happiness, clarity of mind, and stamina to achieve anything you want from now on.

On the other hand, if you continue to eat badly, do not drink enough water, and get very little exercise, then you will find it more difficult to change your life in a truly meaningful way. I'm not saying it will be impossible, but it will certainly be more difficult. It's really the difference between coasting along slowly or speeding along in the fast lane and enjoying the thrill of life.

Food Intolerances

In recent decades, more and more people seem to have allergies to the food that they eat, with gluten, dairy products, and sugar being big contributors to a huge variety of problems.

Foods that contain gluten, daily, and sugar can create a wide variety of symptoms and prevent your body and mind from working at optimum efficiency. And when your body and mind are depleted in energy and vitality, it will slow up the achievement of any goals that you set.

Gluten: Many people are now gluten-intolerant, and gluten affects them negatively in several different ways. It is very possible that giving up foods that contain gluten could improve your health considerably, especially if you often experience gas, bloating, diarrhoea, or constipation.

Also, gluten intolerance can make you feel tired a lot of the time, or give you brain fog, especially after eating a meal that contains gluten. Symptoms can also include dizziness, migraines, and hormone imbalances. Some people who have gluten intolerance even experience more serious conditions like chronic fatigue syndrome, fibromyalgia, anxiety, depression, mood swings, ADD and swelling or pain of the joints — such as fingers, knees, or hips.

Dairy Products: Did you know that humans are the only species that drinks the milk of another animal? When you consider it more deeply, its seems very strange that we drink milk that was meant only for the offspring of cows. Today, a very large proportion of the population have found that dairy products cause them to suffer from a variety of problems. Lactose intolerances can include such common symptoms as bloating, pain or cramps in the lower belly, a build-up of gas, diarrhoea, and even vomiting. Even though you may not experience any of these conditions, dairy products can cause several other problems too.

For example, for most of my adult life, I have found that dairy products give me excessive mucus and congestion and this can even result in painful sinus infections. Sometimes I even start wheezing after eating eat ice cream. Therefore, you might consider cutting out dairy products from your diet for a few weeks, and seeing whether you experience any improvements in your health and wellbeing.

Processed Refined Sugar: Many years ago, my grandfather used to tell me that white sugar was really "the white death". I was only a child at the time, and like most kids I loved sugar, and anything sweet so I didn't take his words very seriously.

However, he was absolutely correct, because refined white sugar causes a huge number of problems for people. We all know the feeling we get whenever we drink a bottle of coke or eat a bar of chocolate. Sugar seems to give us a burst of energy and wellbeing, but after every peak there is always a trough, and later we can end up feeling very tired and even lose our ability to focus.

Sugar really is the single worst ingredient in our modern diet, and it can have harmful effects on our body, its metabolism, and it can contribute to all sorts of diseases. When people eat a lot of products that contain sugar, it can become a major problem and contribute to nutrient deficiencies.

It can also result in increased weight and obesity, because the body cannot eliminate it properly, and also for the simple fact that sugar actually makes you want to eat more food. When people consume too much sugar, it can also cause resistance to the hormone insulin, and result in several diseases including diabetes. There is even evidence to suggest that due to its harmful effects on the metabolism, high sugar consumption could contribute to cancer. Sugar is also highly addictive, because it releases a large amount of dopamine in the brain.

For many years, people have blamed saturated fat as being responsible for heart disease, which is the number one killer throughout the world. However, new studies are now showing that sugar, not fat, may be the leading contributor to heart disease, due to its harmful effects on our entire metabolism.

Therefore, it might be wise for you to consider getting allergy tested and discover if any of the foods you currently consuming, are having any adverse effects on you. By cutting out foods that are not good for you, particularly processed foods, your health could improve dramatically, and you could have more energy, clarity of mind, focus and brain power.

The food that you eat really can have a dramatic effect on your physical, mental, and emotional wellbeing. These in turn have enormous effects on everything else in your life, especially how fast you can achieve your goals.

Nutritional Supplements

Unfortunately, the quality of food that we eat today is different to what it was 50 or 100 years ago. This is mainly due to intensive farming techniques and the widespread use of pesticides and fertilisers. While our fruit and vegetables may look beautiful, unless they are grown organically, their nutritional value may be quite low.

Our physical body repairs itself and heals itself only when we give it the building blocks it need to do its work. However, if the food that we eat does not contain all the building blocks that our body needs, and particularly if those foods are processed and contain additives to extend their shelf life, then our entire system may work a lot less efficiently.

In an ideal world, there would be no need for nutritional supplements. Sadly, due to the way we grow our food today, it may be necessary for you to consider taking nutritional supplements – supplements that will support the healthy functioning of your body and brain.

Therefore, if you are not already getting adequate nutrition from your food, then you may consider taking nutritional supplements that can give your body what it needs to function correctly. This also includes nutrients that are needed by your brain.

Speeding up Your Metabolism

If you are not currently getting regular exercise, then it may be helpful to find something that you really love doing that will help you to get the exercise that you need.

I don't normally enjoy strenuous physical exercise, so I can understand if you don't either — but it's vital that you motivate yourself to do at least some form of regular exercise. For example, I love walking in nature, and sometimes going for a cycle, so it's possible you might find enjoyment in these too. Getting out into nature is great for your body and mind, and you will gain a lot more energy and stamina as a result.

If you really don't enjoy exercise, then just start small and gradually build up to a routine that works well for you. It's never a good idea to go from being completely physically inactive to suddenly running a marathon – unless of course you are being chased by a lion! Starting small and gradually building your stamina will probably be a lot more effective for you. Any improvements that you make in this area will give you benefits that far outweigh the efforts involved.

If you want to perform at a high level, and achieve far more than most people ever do, then you must ensure that you start taking better care of your physical body. The result is that you will have more energy, and the ability to think more clearly, and be more creative. You will also be a lot more efficient, and you will be able to get more done — with a lot less stress.

The Importance of Adequate Sleep

Many well-known entrepreneurs and billionaires start their work day very early in the morning, often many hours before other people arrive at the office. It would be easy to assume that they are "productivity machines" that require almost no sleep.

However, this is rarely the case, and if you probe a little deeper, you will find that many of these highly successful people go to bed a lot earlier than most people.

Many people ignore the importance of getting adequate sleep, and insist that they can perform well after only five or six hours each night. However, according to experts at Harvard Medical School, a consistent lack of sleep can have very negative effects, and it can even be dangerous.

Few people realise that a consistent lack of sleep is also associated with long-term health consequences, including chronic medical conditions such as high blood pressure, diabetes, and heart disease. These conditions could also lead to a shortened life expectancy. A long-term lack of sleep (less than six hours each night) can also lead to obesity, and this in turn can even reduce

"Coffee must make you sleepy. They're always sleepy when they drink it."

the size of your brain. Likewise, too much sleep is not good for you either, and if you habitually sleep for more than nine hours each night, you could also suffer from poor health.

Interestingly, most highly successful people – those that perform at the very highest levels of achievement — get more sleep than you may imagine. They realise that for their body and mind to be able to work at a consistently high level, they have no option but to get adequate sleep so that their body and mind are fully rejuvenated.

Research has shown that most people need between seven and nine hours sleep each night if they want to consistently perform at high levels and achieve the very best results in their daily lives. It's simply not possible to consistently achieve remarkable results in your life if you are sacrificing your sleep time.

If you normally get less than seven hours sleep, you should consider extending your sleep time. You can do this gradually over a few weeks until you are getting more than the recommended minimum of seven hours per night.

Summary:

> **Increasing your brain power** — The food you eat, the water you drink, and the exercise you do directly influence your brain and what you can achieve.

> **Health body – healthy mind** — To achieve your goals more easily, you need to improve these areas: circulation, assimilation, relaxation, and elimination.

> **Food intolerances** — It's possible that you have food allergies that could be slowing you down. Get tested and know for sure!

> **Nutritional supplements** — Due to modern farming techniques, your food may be lacking in nutritious value. Supplementation can help give your body what it needs.

> **Exercise and sleep** — For your body and mind to work effectively, you need to get adequate exercise and get between seven and nine hours sleep each night.

STEP 6: Be a High Performer

Time is the most precious thing you have in your life, because you can use it to make improvements in your own life and in the lives of others.

After all, you only have 24 hours in each day, 365 days in each year, and only so many years in your lifetime.

The reason why most people don't achieve great things in their lives is because they put off to a later time what they could do today. Sadly, that later time rarely arrives, and years can pass by in frustration and disappointment.

You can try to achieve your goals the slow, hard, painful way by not using an effective **"Top dog or not, you gotta slow down."** goal achievement system, or you can use your time wisely and creatively to transform your life in wonderful new ways.

When you study the world's highest performers — the world's most successful people, you will discover that they use **daily routines and habits** that consistently move them towards success. These daily routines are what separate high performers from people who procrastinate and waste valuable time.

Many people already use some sort of daily routine, and it's not just high performers that take advantage of them. However, a high performer is someone who consistently over the long-term achieves remarkable development and improvements in all areas of their life.

Since time is in very short supply, it makes sense that you learn as much as you can from high performers, so that you can mimic their habits and consistently succeed far-above-standard norms over the long term.

High Performance vs. Peak Performance

Before you mimic the high performers, it's important to know the difference between high performance and peak performance. People who focus on achieving peak performance aim to win once, but often find that they cannot sustain this peak performance state for very long. Naturally, there is always a decline after that peak performance state is reached.

High performance is not about working harder or faster. Nor is it about becoming a multitasking machine. High performance techniques allow you to consistently achieve great results in each area of your life, while reducing your stress, increasing your feelings of well-being, and enhancing your health and vitality.

Therefore, it is far wiser to learn the habits of high performers, so that you can consistently achieve a sustainable state of high performance in all areas of your life. Studies of high performers have found that there are specific routines you can use to consistently achieve far more than most people ever do.

Now I'm now going to share these powerful high performance habits with you to help you to achieve your goals more easily. These are techniques that can transform your life and enable you to achieve far more each day than you may have ever believed possible. You'll also be less stressed, more focused, and remain physically and mentally energised.

Daily Planning

Planning daily activities is one of the simplest and most effective secrets of high performers. They **always plan their daily activities**, because by doing so, they consistently get the very best results.

If you are serious about achieving your goals, then this fact alone should motivate you to create your own routine and stick to it each day.

This will allow you to make the most of your own time, and enable you to get the same results as high performers.

Your daily routine will ensure that you are always moving forwards, and taking consistent actions towards achieving your goals.

Here is an example of a basic daily routine for someone who runs their own business, but who is also serious about achieving their goal of becoming a successful writer:

"Now tell me about your big idea."

9am:	Book writing research (uninterrupted - phone/ social media/e-mail all switched off)
10.00am:	2-Minute refocus break
10.02am:	Book writing/research (continued)
11am:	2-Minute refocus break
11.02am:	Phone calls
12pm:	2-Minute refocus break
12.02pm:	e-Mails
1pm:	Lunch break
2pm:	Business development and sales
3pm:	2-Minute refocus break
3.02pm:	Business development and sales (continued)
4pm:	2-Minute refocus break
4.02pm:	e-Mails
4.30pm:	Staff meeting
5pm:	2-Minute refocus break
5.02pm:	Business performance analysis
5.20pm:	Plan for tomorrow

Block Out Time for Goals

It's interesting to note that high performers always do things in a very different way to poor performers and procrastinators. Highly effective, successful people create new habits such as blocking out time, and they use these to consistently achieve sustained levels of high performance.

If you want to achieve a lot more in your life than most people ever do, then you really must start doing things differently. You need to reserve a certain amount of time each day where you specifically focus on achieving your goals. If you don't do this, then your progress could be a lot slower than you want.

"Let me know if I am distracting you."

Most people are at their most creative first thing in the morning. They feel most alive and find that their best ideas and inspiration come to them at this time. If this is your own experience, then you need to consider blocking out time early in the morning to progress your goals.

For others, it could be while they are driving to and from work, or even late at night when everybody else has gone to bed. The important thing is to be able to write down your ideas and progress your goals at the times you normally feel most alive and creative.

Some of my own best ideas come to me while driving long distance, and I use my phone to record my voice so that those ideas aren't forgotten. However, I normally block out the first couple of hours each day in front of my computer. I use this time to work on my goals such as book writing, creating videos and podcasts, and moving my most important projects forwards.

Depending on your own work commitments, lifestyle, and body rhythms, you need to find a time of the day or night that you can consistently block out in your schedule to progress your goals.

Also, depending on the types of goals that you have, you may need to work on different goals at different times. For example, if the next step towards achieving one of your goals is to make phone calls at a specific time of day, then you need to block out time for this activity.

If you don't block out time and just leave everything to chance, then you will generally find that time just slips by. You'll never seem to get any time to work on your goals, because life will always get in the way. Unless you block out time, you will never get the time!

When you block out time to work on your goals, you also need to minimise distractions as far as you possibly can. This could mean switching off your phone, and avoiding checking your email or social media. Or even telling your family and friends that you won't be available anymore between certain times each day.

How to Win Back Time

You may feel that you don't have the time to set aside to create your future, but if so, you may be mistaken. If you cut out an hour of TV so you can go to bed earlier, this means you can get up earlier and work on your goals for an hour before work. Or you could reduce your one-hour lunch break to 30 minutes, and work on your goals in the other 30 minutes.

A fascinating study conducted by Nielsen found that the average American spends an astonishing five hours and four minutes every day watching TV. That's 1,849 hours every year, or 144,222 hours in an average lifetime. Although it may be hard to believe - that's the same as watching TV continuously both day and night without stopping for more than 16-years!

This is very sad when you consider that if the average person would spend just half of that time trying to improve their life, then their circumstance would radically improve. They would live far happier and more fulfilling lives, and be richer in every sense of the word.

Don't get me wrong, I'm not saying TV is all bad. Everybody needs to relax and recharge at the end of a long tiring day, but from time to time, we do need to consider how we spend much of our time. In other words, you need to be very honest with yourself and decide whether you need to adjust your lifestyle so that you and your loved ones can benefit more fully, or just continue the way you are currently going.

Many people who say they "just don't have any free time" may not be thinking creatively, and may be overlooking all sorts of opportunities where they can save time. They need to look at how they spend each hour of most days to find opportunities for adjustment.

As Lucille Ball once said: *"If you want something done, ask a busy person to do it. The more things you do, the more you can do."*

High performers are expert time managers and have no problem in ruthlessly eliminating activities that do not progress their life goals – their goals for their wealth, family, health, and happiness.

When you start to manage your time better, at first it may appear like you are giving up your freedom, but amazingly, most likely you will find it's completely the opposite. When you eliminate activities that don't really benefit you or your family, you will be left with what's truly the most important.

You will have far more time to create and live your life the way you want it, instead of life creating it for you. You may also be surprised by how much time you have for those activities that really matter most – activities that truly contribute to your happiness and the happiness of your loved ones.

It really is important that you make consistent steady progress towards your goals each day, or you may be disappointed with your results. If you commit to doing this from today onwards, you will probably be astounded by your progress and your results.

Daily Success Planner

Now let's look at how you can create a daily success planner. This will help you to create your own daily routine, and it will assist you in blocking out your time for important activities. It will have a very big impact on your life, providing you actually use it! It will allow you to get more done and more easily, and it can help you to transform your goals into reality, fast.

This daily success planner will help you to block out time in your calendar for specific high-priority activities, and it will make sure that you are consistently taking action towards your goals. You can create this success plan at the beginning of each day, or at the end of each day for the following day.

To create your daily success planner, you need to get a piece of paper and along the top, write down the names of the three most important goals or projects that you are currently working towards. These could be your short, medium, or long-term goals, or a combination of them – whatever your top priorities are right now.

Daily Success Planner Example

Project 1:
New Book

Project 2:
New Podcast

Project 3:
Improve Health

Next, under each project name, write out up to five important things that you need to get done in the near future that will help you progress towards achieving that goal. These are some of the most immediate action steps that you need to take, such as:

1 Niche analysis	1 Create podcast name	1 Exercise
2 Brainstorm titles	2 Cover Art Design	2 Nutritionist
3 Daily writing	3 Equipment	3 Meditation
4 Do publishing course	4 Do podcasting course	4 Allergist
5 Cover design	5 Find guests	5 Weights

Also, if other people are involved in helping you to progress these projects, then you also need to write out the names of the people who you need to contact today who will help you progress them. You then need to write out a list of the people who you are expecting to hear back from today so that you can make progress, such as:

People I need to contact today:	People I'm waiting to hear back from:
1 John C	1 Sam
2 Frank C	2 Tony F
3 Tony B	3 Jason R
4 Mary	4 Susan F
5 Bill K	5 Tina J

Finally, at the bottom of the page, you need to write out your top priorities for today. These are the things that you absolutely must get done today, no matter what, such as:

The main things that I must complete today, no matter what are:
- ➤ Complete Amazon niche analysis
- ➤ Write 7 pages of new book
- ➤ Research podcasting equipment
- ➤ Find designer for book and podcast art
- ➤ Find and make appointment with nutritionist

On the next page, you will find a blank Daily Success Planner template you can use yourself.

It's amazing how powerful such a simple tool can be. It took me 28 years of running my own successful businesses before I discovered this simple yet incredibly effective high performance tool. I only wish I had found it decades earlier, because it would have made my journey a lot easier!

It enabled me to write my first bestseller within only a few months, and to double the sales of my already very successful business in less than a year, and to accomplish all sorts of other really big achievements. Had I not used this daily success planner, then many of these goals would have taken much longer to achieve and the process would have been a lot more difficult.

This daily success planner can help create miracles in your work, your finances, and in every area of your life. It will allow you to achieve anything you want far faster than most people ever can. Make sure you use it every day from now on, and you will be richly rewarded!

Daily Success Planner

Projects / Goals

List the 5 major tasks I must do to move each of these projects forward:

Project 1_____   Project 2_____   Project 3_____
1   1   1
2   2   2
3   3   3
4   4   4
5   5   5

People

People I need to contact today: People I'm waiting to hear back from:
1   1
2   2
3   3
4   4
5   5

Today's Priorities

The main things that I must complete today, no matter what are:

_____

_____

_____

_____

_____

_____

This tool is based on proprietary concepts from Brendon Burchard's High Performance Academy

Many people think that multitasking also enables them to be more efficient, and to achieve greater success. But is this really true?

The Multitasking Myth

Over the past 30 years, I have received dozens of resumes from people wanting to work for my businesses, who claimed that they were excellent multitaskers.

"You are the model for multi-tasking."

Unfortunately, a great myth seems to have built up over the years about multitasking and what it can do. I often hear people bragging about their ability to multitask. This means being able to give their focus to several different things at the same time, or being able to switch between different tasks quickly and easily.

However, the research shows that multitasking makes a person more stressed and a lot less productive – by as much as a staggering 40%. A study from Harvard has found that if we wish to be more effective, we should avoid multitasking as much as possible.

According to this revealing study, when we try to juggle several different tasks simultaneously, we are slower and a lot more inaccurate. It's simply not possible to switch between tasks frequently, and not have it impact heavily on your performance, the quality of your work, and your achievements. If you multitask on a frequent basis, you will already know how taxing it is both mentally and physically. Multitasking is responsible for a dramatic decrease in productivity and a reduction in quality work, and this is the complete opposite of what you want to achieve as a high performer.

The research shows that rather than jobseekers boasting in their resumes about their ability to multitask, they would be far wiser to not mention it at all! To do something well, you need to give it your full attention and focus. The same is true when you are taking daily actions towards achieving your goals.

Although we all need to switch between many different tasks throughout the day, there is a way you can do this that is far more beneficial. In this way, you can become energised and recharged with each task switch, rather than slowly but surely draining yourself of energy, focus, and mental ability. We'll look at this method now.

Staying Focused, Alert and Energised

How you feel has a dramatic effect on what you do and what you can achieve. When your mind is clear, amazing things become possible for you. On the other hand, if you often feel quite sluggish, then you will probably achieve a lot less each day.

Most people also become depleted in energy as they move through their day, and by the end of the working day, they can often feel tired and stressed. Losing energy like this is the

"I've been feeling a lot of work related stress."

natural rhythm of life, unless we know how to replenish our energy *as we move through the course of the day.*

High performance studies have found rather than multitasking, taking short breaks is better for your performance.

By taking short breaks several times throughout the day, you'll find that at the end of each day, you'll have a lot more energy than you used to have and will have accomplished a lot more too.

Each break only needs to be as little as 2 or 3 minutes long, and you need to take it every hour (or at least every 90 minutes). By doing this, you'll be able to maintain a sustained level of high performance in everything that you do.

It's for this very same reason that lectures and classes at universities and schools are always kept within these time windows of our ability to focus. It's just not possible to focus on the same task for long periods of time without it impacting your work. By taking a short break every 60 to 90 minutes, you'll give your mind the ability to recharge and refresh, so you can resume your work with more clarity, focus, energy, and enthusiasm. High performance studies have also shown that by combining these short breaks with gentle energy enhancing physical exercises, the quality of your work and your productivity can improve dramatically.

We only get so much energy each day, and as the day progresses, we use up that energy. However, imagine what it would be like if you could replenish the energy you burn up as you progress through the day. It would mean that at the end of the day, you would still have lots of energy to give to your family and relationships, wouldn't it?

This is absolutely possible when you take regular short breaks throughout your working day – breaks that are specifically designed to energise your body and your mind. They can also increase your motivation and elevate your mood and outlook.

These simple high performance techniques allow you to achieve far more and in less time than more than 90% of the population! This is an incredible opportunity to boost your productivity enormously and enjoy what you are doing far more.

One group of exercises that I particularly recommend for this purpose are Qigong (Chi Kung) exercises, and you will find them enormously beneficial.

Do These Exercises - For Increased Energy and Focus

Qigong is an ancient Chinese practise that combined with more strenuous exercises a few times a week, can have enormous effects on your body and mind.

This Qigong routine can invigorate you in less than 3 minutes, and there are 6 phases to this short group of exercises, but they are very easy to understand and use. While doing these exercises, breath slowly and deeply – in through your nose and out through your mouth.

Phase 1: Firstly, you need to stand up and make both of your hands into cup shapes. In other words, put each hand into a waving position, with fingers together, and slightly curve your fingers forwards by about 45 degrees.

You also need to lift your left leg off the ground. You then need to tap firmly with both cupped hands on each side of your ankle at the same time. Gradually, keep tapping your way up both sides of your left leg, up to your knee, and then right the way up your left leg to the very top.

At this point, your left hand will be tapping your left side of your buttocks. The whole process should take only around 20 seconds, so you don't need to go too slowly. Next you need to swap over and do exactly the same for your right leg.

Phase 2: Now, with both feet on the ground, extend your left arm out in front of you with your palm facing down.

Start tapping firmly with your cupped right hand, on the left-hand side of your torso from your waist, gradually moving upwards to your left underarm.

After about 10 seconds, reverse by extending your right arm with your palm facing down, and start tapping the right-hand side of your torso with your left hand cupped — from your waist up to your right under arm.

Again, this should only take you around 10 seconds to complete.

Phase 3: With both feet on the ground again, cup your right hand and hold your left arm straight out in front of you again, with your palm facing downwards.

Now, start tapping with your right cupped hand — starting at the top of the fingers of your left hand and work your way up your arm to your shoulder and also the back of your shoulder.

You can do this over approximately a 20-second period. At this point, you need to swap over and do the same for your right arm.

Phase 4: Now, with both hands cupped, tap them over both your kidneys in your lower back area at the same time for about 10 seconds.

Phase 5: Next, gently bounce up and down on your toes for around 10 seconds — becoming aware of the additional new energy in your body.

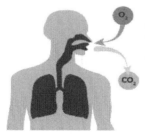

Phase 6: Finally, stand up straight with your legs slightly apart and breathe in rapidly through your nose and out through your mouth.

You should start with gentle breaths, and build up the intensity and speed with each additional breath. Then reverse this by gradually slowing down the speed and intensity of each breath. This exercise takes about 20 seconds to complete.

Likewise, the breathing exercise may make you feel slightly dizzy or lightheaded, so it should also be practised with caution and done very gently at first. I am not a doctor and you should always consult a medical professional before considering trying any new diet or exercise routine.

This short series of exercises will only take you about 3 minutes to complete, but it can give you a lot more energy and renewed focus and even greater clarity of mind. By doing this simple routine every 60 to 90 minutes throughout your working day, you can achieve far more, and in less time than before. This routine will also allow you to get greater enjoyment from your work and help you to achieve all your goals more quickly.

A great way to remind yourself to do these exercises is by setting a reminder on your phone to go off every 60 or 90 minutes. This will ensure that you don't go beyond your ability to focus fully and end up depleting your energy and impairing your mental agility.

Summary:

➤ **Use high performance habits** – Do this to succeed above and beyond standard norms over the long-term, and bring greater happiness and fulfilment into your life.

➤ **Win back time** – Explore how you spend your time, and consider eliminating activities that don't contribute to happiness, wellbeing, or the achievement of your goals.

➤ **Start blocking out time** – Use your Daily Success Planner to ensure you make consistent progress towards all your goals.

➤ **Stop multitasking!** – It ruins your productivity, depletes your energy, and makes you far less effective.

➤ **Use energisation routines** – energise your body and mind every 60 to 90 minutes, thereby reducing stress, increasing stamina, and improving your focus and productivity.

> **Warning:** One of these exercises involves standing on one leg, which may not be suitable for you if you have poor balance or if you're currently overweight, or if you suffer from any condition that could make this exercise a risk for you.

Magnifier: Persistence

Sir Isaac Newton's third law states that *"for every action, there is an equal and opposite reaction"*.

In other words, if you push the wall with your hand, then you feel a force against your hand - this is the wall pushing

"Let's follow the Three P's: Persistence, Patience and Pizza."

back against you with as much force as you apply to it.

Likewise, whenever you start making serious actions towards achieving your goals, you will invoke a direct response from your environment, that is often in proportion to the amount of effort you are making.

In this chapter, we will explore why this happens, and what you can do about it.

Actions Create Changes in Your Environment

When you start taking action to achieve your goals, the first thing you may notice is coincidences starting to happen. Synchronicities that would not have happened if you hadn't taken any action towards achieving your goal. However, you will also invoke a very different kind of response from your environment. No matter what goal you set out to achieve, if it is a big goal, then you must also expect to encounter challenges.

This is like an aeroplane taking off the ground. A modern jet as it hurtles down the runway starts to build up speed. If it were not for the air resistance pushing against its wings, it could not possibly take off into the air. When you start taking serious actions towards achieving your goals, you will experience challenges that may at first make it seem like you are going in completely the wrong direction.

However, with any big goal that you set, there is always a certain amount of inner change that you need to make in order to achieve it. When you experience challenges that stretch your life, it's almost like you qualify yourself, and show you are worthy of achieving that goal. The bigger the goal that you set, the bigger the challenges you will experience. This is nothing to be frightened about, because it is an essential part of achieving your goals.

Challenges Allow You to Achieve Your Goals

The fact is, without challenges that make you grow in certain ways, it's not possible for you to achieve big goals in your life. If you want to achieve everything that you deeply desire, then you must expect challenges along the way. It's these challenges that bring about the changes that are necessary. Without the challenges, nothing much would ever happen.

Sadly, most people give up at the first hurdle. People generally want to find the easy way in all things, but the easy way is certainly not the way

that brings the deepest sense of satisfaction. The easy way brings with it very little sense of achievement or joy, and plenty of dissatisfaction and disappointment.

All the world's most successful people — those who made a big difference — have encountered huge challenges along the way. And if you study their lives, you will see how those very challenges enable them to have such a hugely positive impact on our world. For example, when Thomas Edison was trying to invent the incandescent light bulb, which has lit up our homes for more than a century — he failed 10,000 times! Can you imagine trying to achieve something and failing 10,000 times?! It takes a very special person to develop such persistence.

When Edison was asked about all his failures, he explained that each time he failed, he had found yet another way that the incandescent light bulb would not work — and thus, he was one step closer to achieving his goal. If it were not for Edison's incredible persistence and refusing to give up in the face of failure, then our world would be very different today. His amazing persistence has given the world a very special gift, and has saved innumerable lives in the process.

Do This Exercise: Overcome Challenges and Setbacks

The next time you experience a major challenge that appears to be stopping you from achieving one of your gaols, do this simple exercise. It will give you the motivation and determination you need to keep moving forwards, so that you can overcome the setback.

Remember, behind every wall lies an even greater level of power, wisdom, and riches.

Step 1: Write out 10 negative things you might experience by giving up at this point.

Step 2: Write out 10 benefits you could experience by overcoming this challenge.

Step 3: Write out 10 actions you could take that might help you overcome this challenge.

Step 4: Write out 5 inner qualities you could develop by facing and overcoming this obstacle.

When you do this simple exercise, you will clearly see the huge benefits available to you by not quitting, and by renewing your determination and commitment to succeed.

A quitter never wins and a winner never quits!

Here is a process chart to clarify the exercise:

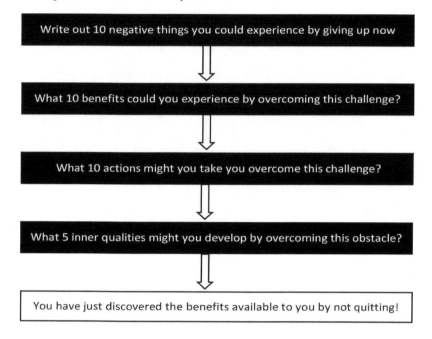

Great Success Is Achieved Through Failure

In fact, failure is almost a prerequisite for success. It is a common trait in most successful people. In almost every case, highly successful people refuse to give up. They are people who have failed far more times than most people, but they have not given up.

True success only comes to those who are persistent and refuse to give in to temporary defeat. If you want to become outrageously successful, then you must refuse to give up and you must keep trying until you succeed!

Christopher Columbus once said that *"by prevailing over all obstacles and distractions, one may unfailingly arrive at his chosen goal or destination."* The word "unfailingly" in this quote is very significant. Columbus is saying here that we cannot fail to achieve our goals when we overcome every obstacle and distraction in our path. What separates those who achieve very little progress in their lives and those who change the world comes down to one thing — and that is persistence.

Here is a story that illustrates this perfectly. It is from Napoleon Hill's *Think and Grow Rich.*

Three Feet from Gold

One of the most common causes of failure is the habit of quitting when one is overtaken by temporary defeat. Every person is guilty of this mistake at one time or another.

In Hill's story, an uncle of R. U. Darby was caught by the gold fever in the gold-rush days, and went west to dig and grow rich. He had never heard that more gold has been mined from the brains of men than has ever been taken from the earth. He staked a claim and went to work with a pick and a shovel. The going was hard, but his lust for gold was definite.

After weeks of labour, he was rewarded by the discovery of the shining ore. He needed machinery to bring the ore to the surface. Quietly, he covered up the mine, retraced his footsteps to his home in Williamsburg, Maryland, and told his relatives and a few neighbours of the "strike". They got together money for the required machinery, and had it shipped. The uncle and Darby went back to work the mine.

The first car of ore was mined, and shipped to a smelter. The returns proved they had one of the richest mines in Colorado! A few more cars of that ore would clear the debts. Then would come the big killing in profits.

Down went the drills! Up went the hopes of Darby and Uncle! Then something happened. The vein of gold ore disappeared. They had come to the end of the rainbow, and the pot of gold was no longer there. They drilled on, desperately trying to pick up the vein again—all to no avail. Finally, they decided to quit.

They sold the machinery to a junk man for a few hundred dollars, and took the train back home. Some "junk" men are dumb, but not this one. He called in a mining engineer to look at the mine and do a little calculating. The engineer advised that the project had failed, because the owners were not familiar with "fault lines". His calculations showed that the vein would be found just three feet from where the Darbys had stopped drilling! And that's exactly where it was found. The "junk" man took millions of dollars in ore from the mine, because he knew enough to seek expert counsel before giving up.

Most of the money that went into the machinery was procured through the efforts of R. U. Darby, who was then a very young man. The money came from his relatives and neighbours, because of their faith in him. He paid back every dollar of it, although he was years in doing so.

Long afterwards, Mr. Darby recouped his loss many times over when he made the discovery that desire can be transmuted into gold. The discovery came after he went into the business of selling life insurance. Remembering that he lost a huge fortune because he stopped three feet from gold, Darby profited by the experience in his chosen work. He did this with the simple method of saying to himself, "I stopped three feet from gold, but I will never stop because men say 'no' when I ask them to buy insurance."

Darby is one of a small group of fewer than fifty men who sell more than a million dollars in life insurance annually. He owes his stickability to the lesson he learned from his quitability in the gold mining business.

Before success comes in any man's life, he is sure to meet with much temporary defeat and perhaps, some failure. When defeat overtakes a man, the easiest and most logical thing to do is to quit. That is exactly what the majority of men do. More than five hundred of the most successful men this country (the United States) has ever known told the author (Napoleon Hill) **their greatest success came just one step beyond the point at which defeat had overtaken them**. Failure is a trickster with a keen sense of irony and cunning. It takes great delight in tripping one when success is almost within reach.

Crisis = Opportunity

Dr Maxwell Maltz once said that a "crisis" is a situation that can either make us or break us. If we react properly to that crisis, it can give us strength, power, and wisdom that we would not ordinarily possess. On the other hand, we can allow that crisis to rob us of the skill, control, and ability that we normally possess.

Likewise, the Chinese character for "crisis" also means "opportunity" and this signifies that every crisis contains within it a great opportunity. Everything comes down to how we react to our changing circumstances and Maltz's observation was that when faced by a crisis, then the best and **quickest way to overcome that crisis is to become far more determined.**

Therefore, whenever you face any crisis that could prevent you from achieving a goal, you should actually be more encouraged than before — simply because you are meeting some resistance. It is actual proof that you are making progress towards your goal!

Example Affirmations for Developing Persistence:
- ➤ I am persistent in achieving my goals.
- ➤ I am always moving forwards no matter what happens.
- ➤ I am naturally persistent and challenges make me even stronger.

Beware — Your Greatest Enemy Lies Within!

Within every person are two types of "inner voice". A "voice" that is loud and insists on being noticed, and a "small quiet voice" that is a lot subtler.

Our negative inner voice is loud and very persistent. It constantly tells us that we are not worthy, or that we don't have what it takes to succeed. It also tells us not to bother, and to take the easy way in everything.

This "negative inner voice", is simply a part of ourselves that tries to sabotage everything we try to create. It's very crafty, and it is well aware of all our vulnerabilities and feelings of

"It's always a good idea to get to know your neighbour."

inadequacy. This negative inner voice uses every Achilles' heel that we possess in order to stop us from improving in our life.

On the other hand, the small quiet voice is the voice of our wisdom. It is the part of our life that is constantly trying to nudge us in the right direction. We need to really listen attentively if we are to hear the wisdom and guidance that it is trying to impart to us. However, what's most important here is to develop the ability to recognise and overcome the influence of our negative inner voice, because it's that voice that holds back most people, and to an incredible extent.

This part of our mind has been created through all the conditioning and painful experiences we have encountered during our life. I have already shared with you ways that can help you to overcome this conditioning. But it's important to realise that no matter how effectively you do this, this negative inner voice can never be completely eradicated.

Our life is a continual struggle between light and dark, positive and negative, wisdom and delusion. Although you can greatly reduce the effects of this negative inner voice, you still need to be aware that it is always within you, and it is always trying its best to interfere in every way that it can. You can remain an ordinary person, or become an extraordinary person. Which one you become is dependent on whether you succeed in overcoming this inner negativity or not.

So how do we reduce the effects of this trickster who constantly gives us all sorts of negative thoughts that try to hold us back? Simply being aware that within you, there is a part of your mind that is working against your goals, this can help you greatly in reducing its influence. Also, by summoning up a burning desire to achieve your goals, the effects of this negativity can be even further reduced.

This negativity works most effectively in people who have no goals in life, or who don't have any clear direction. It keeps such people powerless to change their lives. However, this is definitely not you, because you wouldn't be reading this book if you didn't have big goals, or if there was nothing you wanted to achieve in your life.

By just remaining aware and vigilant of this inner negativity, you will be able to recognise and reduce its effects, and achieve your goals more easily. Dream big, be persistent, and never give in to any obstacles on your path, whether external or internal!

Summary:

> **Challenges allow you to achieve your goals** — They make you more capable and create changes within you that enable you to achieve your goals.
> **Success is often achieved through failure** — Successful people fail more times than unsuccessful people. Failure is often a springboard to success.

- **A crisis is also an opportunity** — It gives you strength, power, and wisdom that you would not ordinarily possess, and it is often critical to goal achievement.
- **You have a negative inner voice** — It tries to sabotage all your goals. You can overcome it by being aware of it, and by summoning up a burning determination.

STEP 7: Overcome Limiting Beliefs

W hat you believe about life and your own capabilities can determine where you are right now in your life. You are the sum of all your beliefs, and if your life is not exactly the way you want it to be, then your beliefs may be responsible.

Beliefs can be very powerful, and they can determine whether you achieve your goals. They can limit your choices in the present and what you can achieve in the future, and even affect how your life turns out.

"Let's try it without the parachute."

Everyone has limiting beliefs of some sort – even those who are already highly successful. Limiting beliefs can prevent you from dreaming big and discovering what you are truly capable of. They can also hold you back from achieving your bigger goals in life – but it doesn't have to be that way.

You can quickly and easily discover what has been holding you back the most. When you have done that, you can overcome these roots of self-sabotage using the strategies, tools, and techniques you'll find in this chapter. Then, you will be able to achieve your goals far more easily than most people ever do.

Your Circumstances Never Define Your Achievements

Highly successful people are those who take full control of their life by choosing how they think – and they think very differently to most people. When you start to question your beliefs about what is possible and when you start to change how you think, then your exterior reality will also start to reflect those changes, and often very quickly.

If I told you that you could have the mind of a millionaire, would you believe me? It's possible that you may believe this, but it's more likely that you may not. But imagine for a moment what would start happening in your life if you really did start thinking like a multi-millionaire. If you could somehow magically start thinking in the same ways that highly successful people think, almost anything would be in your grasp, wouldn't it?

"Hang on for a moment," you might say. "My situation is completely different from people like that. You simply don't understand how it is for me — my situation is totally different."

I'm afraid this is a lie that many people tell themselves, repeatedly. It is a self-limiting belief that is simply not true. Your circumstances never define who you are or what you can become.

Many people also believe that when they make more money, then they will be successful, but this also is not true. Rather, you need to become a successful person and develop a *success mindset first*, and then quite naturally, true riches will start to appear in your life.

Success is therefore the result of adopting a specific mindset, and it is not dependent on what you have in your life right now.

If you take the time to study the world's most successful people, you'll find that in many cases, they started from nothing, and often had very little education. For example, at the beginning of the 20th century, Andrew Carnegie was the richest man in the world. When you adjust for inflation, his net worth today would be over $310 billion. But when you study Carnegie's life, he came from a background of poverty. He arrived in the United States with his family as an immigrant from Scotland.

Slowly but surely, through his own efforts, Carnegie became one of the most successful people in human history, and later in his life he gave away most of his fortune to charities and trusts, some of which exist to this day. Carnegie (like most highly successful people) believed that it was possible for any person to learn all the skills they needed to become successful and deeply fulfilled.

This remarkable man later convinced a young law student called Napoleon Hill to study the lives of highly successful people. His desire was for Hill to bring to the world a true philosophy of success — a philosophy that was so powerful anyone could use it to transform their circumstances and achieve success.

Carnegie arranged lots of introductions for Hill. He introduced Hill to many of the world's most successful people, so that Hill could discover for himself what common traits these highly successful people possessed.

This task took Hill many years to complete, but it resulted in one of the greatest bestsellers of all time. His book *Think and Grow Rich* is still a bestseller today, almost 100 years later, and it has helped millions of people to become successful and achieve remarkable transformations in their lives.

In fact, this amazing book is also the "grandfather" of most modern self-help books and courses on success and achievement. It has influenced almost every thought leader today and its effect on the world has been enormous. No matter what courses or seminars on success you may have attended, or what books on goal setting and wealth you have read, it will have been greatly influenced by Hill's *Think and Grow Rich*.

Since your circumstance do not define what you can achieve, the only things that are stopping you right down from achieving your life's biggest goals, are your current thoughts and beliefs. And when you start to change them, much more will become possible for you, and your life will start to change very quickly!

The Power of Belief

Our entire outlook on life is based on our belief system. Our whole concept of the universe and our place in it is formed through our beliefs, and it is ourselves who have chosen these beliefs.

Our beliefs are the things we choose to think are true, based on the information and experiences we have been exposed to during our lives.

However, just because we believe something is true doesn't necessarily mean that it is!

For example, when I was very young my dad was on TV, and I will never forget the days that led up to his first TV appearance. Most kids would be excited and proud to know their dad would be on TV, especially back in the 1960s when many people in Ireland still didn't have a TV. However, I was totally petrified!

I had overheard a conversation between my dad and my grandfather, where my grandfather had asked my dad if the TV studio would be shooting him live. My father replied no, that he wouldn't be live. To a kid who had only seen a TV two or three times, this obviously meant that the studio would be shooting him dead!

"Would the TV camera really shoot him? It certainly looked like it..."

I mean, if they're going to be shooting you, which is already a pretty scary thought, and especially if you're not going to be live, then obviously they're going to be shooting you dead, aren't they?!

I was in a living hell, and the night my dad left our home to go to the TV studio, I was shaking with fear that I would never see him alive again. I got very little sleep that night, but happily, my dad was fine when I got up the following morning.

The only thing that kept my hope alive was that my mum didn't seem at all worried about his TV appearance, and seemed perfectly normal – though still I wasn't quite sure what was going to happen. I really did think the TV camera might kill him! Isn't it amazing what we can end up believing when we are missing important information?

Many years later, I worked as a hospice volunteer, and every Wednesday I supported and talked with people in their last days of physical life. When people know that they won't be alive much longer, they can become very peaceful or very agitated. I remember one of the patients who was very close to the end, and in his last few days, he became absolutely terrified – he was petrified that there might be nothing after death and that very soon his life and consciousness would be completely annihilated.

I shared with him my many years of research into near death experiences and the evidence for life after death. I explained to him that although I'm very scientifically minded and sceptical, having studied and researched this subject for many years, I have discovered an incredible amount of solid evidence (much of it scientific-based) that life continues after physical death.

I shared with him some of this research, and the effect on him was startling. He became peaceful and reassured, and when I went to go, he gripped my hand and thanked me profusely. He died peacefully that night, believing that his life would survive his physical death.

Isn't it amazing how our beliefs can affect us so powerfully? However, just because you believe something, it doesn't mean that it's real – in fact, we all believe many things that aren't based on fact.

As you move through life and experience new things, your beliefs generally start to change. For example, what you believe today may be completely different to what you believed when you were a child. Even so, when you encounter strong evidence showing you that your deepest-held beliefs are incorrect, then it can sometimes feel like your entire world is crumbling. When your entire belief system has been challenged, it can be deeply traumatic, and you can end up feeling lost and out of control.

This is the reason why many people who are presented with direct evidence that a deep-seated long-held belief is incorrect will often still cling to that belief, and even more powerfully than before. They can become angry and defensive to protect themselves from having to completely re-evaluate what they have based their life on for so many years.

Even if they discover that their beliefs about life are incorrect, they may still ignore the evidence and continue to live their life just like before. The saying "ignorance is bliss" is true in so many ways — it can be very painful for people to face the truth, because this means they will probably need to change their life in some way. And to be perfectly honest, most people don't want to change, because it requires effort.

Beliefs Can Kill

Beliefs can be so powerful that they can even kill you! There have been cases where a patient has been misdiagnosed by their doctor, and have been told that they are suffering from a terminal illness and only have six months to live. Even

though the diagnosis may be completely incorrect, and this may be verified later by autopsy, people who have been told that they have only six months to live often die after exactly that six-month period has elapsed.

"Tomorrow I'll teach you how to land."

Once they have been given the dreadful news, they become depressed and resigned to their fate. With each passing week, their energy starts to decline. Their negative thoughts, beliefs, and expectations start creating changes in their body that slowly but surely kills them.

Likewise, there have been many cases where people have overcome life-threatening diseases by adopting a positive, empowering attitude, and by refusing to be defeated. Such apparent miracles often happen when there is a deep need to survive, for example, caring for loved ones who are completely dependent on them.

Question Your Beliefs

Your beliefs too have profound effects on your physical body and indeed all aspects of your life. The beliefs that you hold are a mixture of empowering beliefs and disempowering beliefs, and they dictate what you can and cannot achieve. But at some point, you need to ask yourself where many of your beliefs actually came from.

Many of our beliefs are formed through our own direct experiences and disappointments, but a large proportion of them are handed down to us from our parents, relatives, and friends. It's really no wonder why many of us suffer and struggle so much in our lives.

We are all walking around in a self-created prison of the mind that is based upon inaccurate ways of thinking. We absorbed these erroneous ways of thinking like osmosis from people who were also imprisoned by their own mind – and we may not even realise it!

For example, most people have certain religious beliefs, views on marriage, political affiliations, favourite sports teams, views on racism, and many other viewpoints — simply because when they were young they were surrounded by people who believed in these things. When a child doesn't know any better, it just copies the adults around it.

As a result, we all have a mixture of beliefs that are both right and wrong, and we have even created stories and reasoning in our mind to justify why those beliefs are right or wrong. The truth is, however, that most people never really look at why they believe such stories to be true in the first place. So, a great proportion of our outlook on life and what we believe has been absorbed at a young age from those around us.

You have within you right now all sorts of extraordinary abilities and potential to create the life you have always wanted to live. But you also have many thoughts and beliefs that are holding you back. These thoughts and beliefs are continually sabotaging all your chances of success. Unless you do something about it that is!

Your Conditioning Is Holding You Back

The fact is, we all carry within us beliefs that hold us back. We have all been conditioned to think in certain ways, to believe certain things, and to act in certain ways.

It's not possible to live a single day in this world without being conditioned by our environment in some way. This has resulted in so many problems throughout the world, and it's the reason why otherwise extraordinary people remain powerless, and are never able to achieve their goals in life.

You may feel that there is very little conditioning holding you back, but I assure you that there is. Whether you believe it or not, your thoughts, beliefs, and emotions determine whether you will succeed at anything you try to achieve. Even the world's most successful people have been conditioned.

Uncovering and overcoming our conditioning and self-limiting beliefs is important if we want to achieve anything truly remarkable in our lives. What makes an ordinary person become extraordinary is down to whether they succeed in uncovering and overcoming their self-limiting beliefs.

Right now, you carry within you all sorts of attitudes, beliefs, and conditioning that are holding you back from living the life that you could be living. If this were not the case, then you would have already achieved all your life's biggest goals. You would already have been able to get whatever you wanted from life, and you would not be reading this book.

Right now, you may believe that you are not worthy, not intelligent enough, not attractive enough, that you don't have enough resilience, that you are not determined enough, or that you simply don't have what it takes to succeed. Some of your beliefs may be correct, but that doesn't mean you can't change these things. And many of your beliefs are far from being true, and probably hold you back in more ways than you can possibly imagine.

If you want to achieve your biggest goals in life, then you must have a way to root out and uncover the conditioning that is holding you back. Fortunately, I have some great news for you. It's possible to discover what beliefs you are carrying right now that are holding you back from achieving your goals. And when you find out what these erroneous beliefs are, you can loosen their grip on your life — and more easily than you may imagine.

When you overcome these self-limiting beliefs, it will almost feel like you are reborn. It's like sweeping the slate clean, and starting afresh without any impediments in your way. What was difficult before now becomes easy, and you will finally realise that you really can achieve whatever you want in life.

You Can Change Your Life

It really is quite remarkable what can start happening in your life when you start making changes within yourself. Earlier I shared with you the struggles I experienced myself during my first few years of business, which were a result of my low self-worth and poor self-esteem. However, when I uncovered this self-sabotage and started doing something about it, my business started to thrive and I became very successful.

For many years, I spent only a day and a half working each week, while devoting most of my time and energy to voluntary work. Everything changed for me as soon as I started overcoming the deep-seated beliefs I had about myself, my capabilities, and my self-worth.

I changed from being a person who had very little self-confidence into someone who could appear on radio and TV without losing his nerve. I gradually moved from being someone who felt they had no purpose in life to becoming someone who felt a deep sense of purpose, and who desired to help other people in a very significant way. Also, I changed from being a person who didn't value their own time into someone who truly values their own time and the preciousness of other people's time.

I moved from being someone who didn't value money and was always broke to selling my highly successful company to a multinational. And as I started to respect myself more, I found that I had a lot more respect for other people too. I promise you can do this too.

"Therapy is wonderful. Finally to have someone who pays attention to my self esteem issues."

You could go through years of psychotherapy to discover what's holding you back, but I think you'll agree that your time is a lot more valuable than that! There are all sorts of methods you can use to discover the negative subconscious beliefs that you hold. It's also possible to use hypnosis to achieve the same result and a lot more quickly.

You can overcome the beliefs that are preventing you from achieving great success and happiness and are sabotaging all your chances of achieving your goals.

As you start to change, you will develop a power within you that is truly unstoppable and your environment will start reflecting those changes too. The result of this can be a major transformation in all your circumstances.

So now let's explore a simple, effective method that will quickly allow you to root out and overcome these blocks to your success. And it's a method that can give you results within the next hour!

Do This Exercise: Uncover and Overcome Your Limiting Beliefs

The English language contains a wonderful word that can help you to uncover all sorts of limiting beliefs. That word is "because", and whenever you see the word "because" in a sentence, it is always followed by a reason.

This means you can use the word "because" as a tool to uncover all sorts of reasons — both conscious and subconscious — why you cannot achieve something. I know this may sound simplistic, but keep reading and you will see just how powerful this is.

In this exercise, you will be reading a sentence about not being able to achieve something, and you will be reading that sentence aloud. Then you will write out 10 reasons why you cannot achieve it.

You need to do the first part of this exercise as quickly as you can without really thinking. Don't be logical, just read the sentence aloud, and write down your first reason as quickly as you can. You need to just write down the first thing that comes into your mind, no matter how crazy it may seem.

This exercise is **not** about coming up with logical reasons. Rather, it is an exercise you need to do as quickly as possible, without really thinking, or analysing or even judging your reasons. When you do this, some of those reasons will be coming directly from your subconscious mind.

It's your subconscious beliefs and attitudes that we want to reveal in this exercise. If you do the first part of this exercise slowly, then it will **not** work nearly as well for you.

On the other hand, when you write the very first thing that comes into your mind, without even thinking or analysing it in anyway, your results may be very revealing.

Here are each of the steps in this exercise in more detail, and in this case we are uncovering limiting beliefs about wealth:

Step 1: Speak the following sentence out loud *"I can't become rich because......."*

Step 2: Next, as quickly as you can write out a single reason why you can't become rich.

Step 3: Next, speak the same sentence aloud again *"I can't become rich because......."* and quickly write out another reason why you can't become rich. Repeat this exact same process (of reading the sentence aloud and quickly writing your response) until you have at least 10 reasons.

Step 4: Now look at each of your reasons, and you may be surprised by what they reveal!

If you are currently not rich and you believe it may be difficult to become wealthy, then I'm sure you have written down all sorts of valid reasons why that is so. It's easy to come up with lots of reasons why you can't achieve something, particularly if it's a big, long-term goal.

For example, you might come up with some of the following reasons that could show you the unhealthy attitudes and beliefs you currently hold towards money and wealth.

I can't become rich because:
- ➤ Money doesn't grow on trees
- ➤ Rich people are greedy

> ➤ If I was wealthy, everybody would hate me
> ➤ There is only so much to go around
> ➤ Money is the root of all evil
> ➤ Rich people are smart, and I'm not
> ➤ Rich people are arrogant
> ➤ It will be too hard to achieve

Please make sure you have at least 10 responses before you complete this first step of the process. If you want to keep going and can come up with 20 or 30 answers, then it could make this technique even more effective.

Scoring:

Next, look at each response that you have written and give yourself a mark from 1 to 10 for each one. If a response has a strong feeling attached to it, then give it a mark between 6 and 10 – the stronger the emotion, the higher your rating. On the other hand, the responses that you don't really believe or that don't have a strong feeling attached to them — mark between 1 and 5.

You are looking for the responses that have the most emotional charge associated with them. The ones that you feel most strongly about, even if you cannot rationally explain why.

So, go through your list of responses and score each one. Those responses that scored between 7 and 10 are most likely the attitudes and beliefs that are currently holding you back the most.

For this example, I have included sample ratings for each response as follows:

I can't become rich because:
> ➤ Money doesn't grow on trees SCORE: 1
> ➤ Rich people are greedy **SCORE: 7**
> ➤ If I was wealthy, everybody would hate me **SCORE: 7**
> ➤ There is only so much to go around SCORE: 3
> ➤ Money is the root of all evil SCORE: 3
> ➤ Rich people are smart, and I'm not **SCORE: 9**
> ➤ Rich people are arrogant SCORE: 5
> ➤ It will be too hard to achieve **SCORE: 10**

Those highlighted in bold are the scores of four beliefs that could possibly have the greatest emotional charge. Of course, your own scoring may be completely different from the examples.

Create Your List of Opposites:
The next step in this technique is to create a new list of responses, but this time you are creating beliefs that are the complete opposite to the previous ones. Also, for this step only select those with the 4 highest scores / the highest emotional charge.

This time, you can take as much time as you like to come up with reasons that counteract those 4 beliefs with the highest emotional charge, as you are no longer trying to draw forth your subconscious beliefs. Rather, you are trying to do the complete opposite – discover logical reasons that will cancel out your limiting subconscious beliefs.

Write out as many opposite reasons as you can for each of these 4 limiting beliefs, and again the more you can come up with the better. The effect that this will have is to loosen the grip these limiting beliefs currently have over you.

Eliminate Those with the Least Emotional Charge:
When you have written out these counteracting beliefs for each of your four limiting beliefs with the highest scores, start eliminating those with the least emotional charge.

Remove each one until you have a single powerful empowering belief to counteract each one of your four limiting beliefs.

So, in the previous example, these are the four beliefs with the highest emotional charge. In other words, the limiting beliefs with the most potential negative effects on your life and achievements.

I can't become rich because:
- ➤ Rich people are greedy **SCORE: 7**
- ➤ If I was wealthy, everybody would hate me **SCORE: 7**
- ➤ Rich people are smart, and I'm not **SCORE: 9**
- ➤ It will be too hard to achieve **SCORE: 10**

And here are examples of the best opposite beliefs we have come up with for each of them.

I <u>CAN</u> become rich because:

➤ Rich people are generous and contribute to society

➤ When I am wealthy, I will have more time to help others, who will appreciate me

➤ I can easily learn how other people became rich and copy what they did

➤ It's easy for me to attract wealth, because I choose thoughts of gratitude and abundance

Create Affirmations for a Success Mindset:

The final step in this process is to convert these empowering new beliefs into affirmations that counteract the limiting beliefs that you have uncovered.

Your final list will be very helpful in creating the affirmations that will help you to reprogram your subconscious mind and overcome the limitations that have been holding you back.

As you may remember from the earlier section on affirmations, you need to write them in the present tense. They also need to be positive, personal, and specific.

Now, let's convert these new empowering beliefs above into affirmations, which you can add to the affirmations you are already doing each day. You also need to read your affirmations aloud when you wake up in the morning and before going to sleep each night, while triggering your GA.

Here is one way we can write the empowering beliefs as affirmations:

➤ I am rich and generous and love contributing to society

➤ I am wealthy, and have lots of time to help others, who appreciate me

➤ I am learning from rich people and become even richer myself

➤ I am attracting wealth easily, and I choose thoughts of gratitude and abundance

As these are only examples, you need to do this exercise fully yourself to discover your own self-limiting beliefs. You can then create opposite beliefs and convert those beliefs into affirmations that cancel out your limiting beliefs and their effects on your life.

Of course, the example for wealth and money is only one important area of your life that you need to explore. You may also need to examine your deep-seated attitudes and beliefs in several other areas, for this process to be truly effective and deeply transformational.

Let's look at a few other examples, you might consider. These are from a variety of areas of your life, where you could have several limiting beliefs.

I can't succeed in life because…

Regarding my life, I feel:
> ➤ sad because…
> ➤ angry because…
> ➤ ashamed because…
> ➤ guilty because…
> ➤ afraid because…

You can also create your own sentences based on what you want to achieve. For example, if you want to discover some of the things that are holding you back from achieving your goals, you might create a sentence like this: *Regarding my goals, I can't achieve them because…*

Again, once you have identified the main limiting beliefs that are currently holding you back, you can select the four that are the most emotionally charged, so that you can start working to counteract their effects on your life.

Just like in the previous example, you then need to find the most powerful opposite belief you can create for each one of them — the very best reason you can think of why it may be true, and then convert it into a powerful affirmation that will reprogram your subconscious mind.

You can also use these affirmations in your subliminal programs and self-hypnosis sessions for even greater effect. The more impressions you make on your subconscious mind, the quicker and easier it will be to overcome your limiting beliefs.

This way, you can overcome decades of conditioning and the long-term negative effects of painful experiences so that you can finally throw off the shackles that have held you back for so many years.

The only way that you can take a giant leap forward and achieve your life's biggest goals is to do this exercise and start reprogramming your mind for success. This single step has the power to completely transform your life in ways that may appear miraculous to you.

Do not delay doing this exercise — do this step right now, and see what happens for yourself!

See process chart on the next page:

Summary:

➤ **You have been conditioned** — Other people and what you have experienced have conditioned you.

➤ **Your circumstances never define who you are or what you can become.**

➤ **Your beliefs are powerful** — They determine what you experience.

➤ **Your subconscious beliefs hold you back** — They also constantly sabotage your success.

➤ **You can change your beliefs** — By doing so, your circumstance will also change.

➤ **Uncover your limiting beliefs** — Do this using the "because" technique.

➤ **Overcome those limiting beliefs** — By creating opposite beliefs and converting them into affirmations that program your mind for success, you can overcome limiting beliefs.

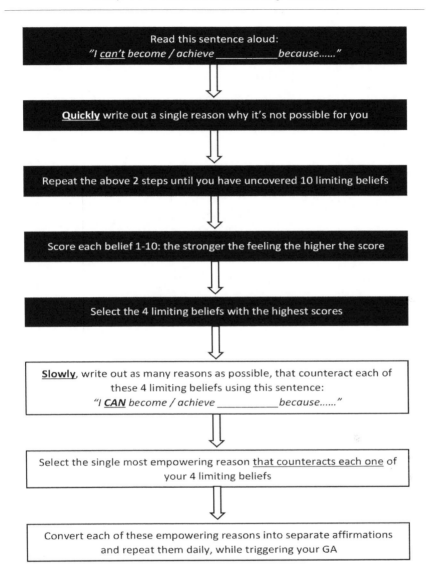

Read this sentence aloud:
"I *can't* become / achieve _____ because......"

Quickly write out a single reason why it's not possible for you

Repeat the above 2 steps until you have uncovered 10 limiting beliefs

Score each belief 1-10: the stronger the feeling the higher the score

Select the 4 limiting beliefs with the highest scores

Slowly, write out as many reasons as possible, that counteract each of these 4 limiting beliefs using this sentence:
"I **CAN** become / achieve _____ because......"

Select the single most empowering reason that counteracts each one of your 4 limiting beliefs

Convert each of these empowering reasons into separate affirmations and repeat them daily, while triggering your GA

Magnifier: Lifelong Learning

There is just one guarantee in life, and that is that **nothing ever remains the same.** Everything in the universe is in a constant state of flux. Likewise, the age we now live in is bringing us more changes, and at a greater speed than at any other time in human history.

The Industrial Revolution changed our world completely and in a relatively short time. During this period, people moved from villages and rural areas into towns and cities in search of work.

In the past few years, however, due to the ability to work remotely, many people are now moving away from cities and back into rural areas once again.

But these are tiny changes compared to what's on the very near horizon. We are now on the brink of a new revolution, a revolution that will change humanity like never before, and its impact may even be greater than the industrial revolution was. And this revolution will cause many people to suffer greatly unless they start taking immediate action.

Your Job May Be Under Threat

We are now entering the age of robotics and artificial intelligence, and your job may be under threat very soon. Oxford University researchers have estimated that 47% of jobs in the United States could be automated within the next two decades.

Some researchers suggest far higher figures due to the exponential speed of change we are experiencing in all areas of technology.

For example, in the past 10 years alone, we have learned more about the human brain then we have in the entire history of the human race. Combine this with breakthroughs in medicine, quantum physics, and the field of electronics, and we may find that changes become a lot quicker and more radical than we can possibly imagine.

Studies into the impact of robotics and artificial intelligence often focus on the effects they will have on manual labour, and some studies even suggest that 90% of certain types of manual jobs will be replaced by robotics and artificial intelligence in the next 5 to 10 years. Different studies come up with different estimates, but it's impossible to deny that we are on the verge of a massive transformation in the way work is carried out.

"Well, one thing Is for sure... they'll never replace doctors with robots."

Unless people start to learn new skills, many will find themselves unemployed in the not-too-distant future. However, it's not just manual jobs that are under threat from these new technologies. <u>Every type of employment will be affected to some extent.</u>

Even people with college degrees and professional degrees like lawyers are doing things that are predictable, and a lot of these jobs will also be susceptible over time.

This means that if we are to survive the coming robotics revolution, remain employed, become successful, and achieve our life's biggest goals, then we must learn new skills — and quickly.

At this point, the most at-risk jobs appear to be in the areas of data collection, data processing, and predictable physical work, particularly if they are in these areas:

➤ Accommodation and food services
➤ Manufacturing
➤ Agriculture
➤ Transportation and warehousing
➤ Retail trade
➤ Mining
➤ Construction
➤ Utilities
➤ Wholesale trade
➤ Arts, entertainment, and recreation

A lot of activities that normally only take up a short amount of time in the workplace will also be automated, particularly in the following sectors:

➤ Managing others
➤ Applying expertise
➤ Stakeholder interactions
➤ Unpredictable physical work

This means that if you are affected by these changes, you only have a finite window of opportunity to change the direction of your career so you will be protected from unwanted influences, and you can truly be the master of your own destiny.

Online Learning

Fortunately, there is another wonderful revolution taking place at the same time, and it is taking place online. It's now possible to learn almost any new skill quickly and easily thanks to all sorts of online learning websites. Websites like Udemy.com are enabling ordinary people to learn new skills from some of the world's greatest teachers and educators, and in the comfort of their own home.

Distance learning has been available for over 100 years in the form of home study and correspondence courses. However, you can now learn virtually any new skill online, and in a way that is much easier than ever before. Today, complex technical skills can easily be demonstrated through video, audio, interactive webinars, and downloadable materials.

One of the many benefits of online learning is that it's normally considerably cheaper than going to university. Also, you can learn what you need at your own pace, rather than having to take time off work to do a more formal course.

When you do an online course, you're never alone. You often have a group of fellow students who you have access to, as well as the tutors themselves. This allows you to interact with students and educators, and get all your questions answered. This makes it far easier to learn new skills, and more quickly.

The fact remains that if you are not updating your skills, or learning new skills, then you could be left far behind in the not-too-distant future. We truly are entering the era when continual lifelong learning will be essential.

Back in 1987 when I started my first business, I learned everything the hard way. My learning was based on trial and error, and I read very few books about business. I felt that business books were boring, and I would avoid them like the plague. Over the following 14 years, I grew that business to a substantial size, and eventually sold it to a multinational in 2001.

Looking back, I now realise that I could have grown that business much more quickly, and to an even larger size, had I made the effort to improve my skills. I simply did not learn from other people who had achieved success, and who could have helped me greatly along my own journey to success.

It was only a few years later — after making bad investments, by trusting the wrong people, and after losing all my fortune that I truly discovered the true importance of lifelong learning. I was in a truly desperate situation, and I had to learn new skills really fast if my family and I were to survive. I remember spending my last 10 Euros on food — it was really that bad. I realised that if things were to change for us, I had to learn new skills that I had never possessed before.

It was at exactly this time that I started learning about the importance of mentors. In other words, learning from people who had already achieved what I wanted to achieve — because success is actually a learned behaviour. You too could also benefit greatly by having a mentor.

Success Is a Transferrable Skill

In the Far East, there is a concept known as the mentor-disciple relationship. Most people in Asia understand this concept as being a vital necessity to achieve anything worthwhile in life. However, in the Western world, it seems completely alien to us. However, it is a concept that can enable you to transform your life very quickly.

In the West, the nearest we may come to seeing this mentor-disciple relationship in action is to look at the relationship between a master craftsman and his apprentice. Every master craftsman had an outstanding teacher. It's just not possible to master any complex skill on your own unless you have decades to do so, or have an excellent teacher to guide you.

If you want to excel at anything, you must have an outstanding teacher — a teacher who has already achieved what you wish to achieve. There is simply no need to reinvent the wheel. If you want to become highly successful in any area of life or business, all you need to do is seek out someone who has already achieved great success in that field. You need to learn from them, and copy what they did to achieve their success. This is the fastest and most direct route to achieving anything significant and worthwhile.

Back in my own dark days of great loss, I started learning from some of the world's most successful people, as well as top internet marketing experts, marketing gurus, and motivational speakers. I literally immersed myself in all sorts of new skill sets that I desperately needed to learn.

However, it's important to understand that learning for the sake of learning is pretty much useless. Rather, you should only focus on learning whatever is required for the next step towards achieving your goal. There is a saying "just in time learning" that explains this concept clearly.

On the other hand, if you just cram your head full of all sorts of stuff, and you don't start implementing it immediately, then you could have wasted a lot of valuable time.

Learn Only What You Can Use Right Now

True benefit comes when we learn a new skill and **immediately put that learning into practice**. That way, we can make real tangible progress towards our goals. It also means that we truly understand what we have learned, and we will remember all the experiences associated with it.

We cannot truly say we have learned something unless we have actually put it into practice — <u>understanding only comes after we take action</u>. I honestly believe it is a great crime to learn valuable new skills and never use them to benefit other people.

Also, there is a saying that "knowledge is power", but it is actually nothing of the sort. **Knowledge only becomes power when it is acted upon and used**. Knowledge without action is completely powerless and in many cases, it can be a complete waste of time. That's why it's important to be very selective in what you learn, and only learn from teachers who are truly outstanding, and who have already achieved the goal you have set for yourself.

Mentors Can Transform Your Life

We all have limiting beliefs — beliefs that hold us back from achieving our biggest goals. If we allow those beliefs to perpetuate, then we can be held back in many areas of our life. On the other hand, by seeking out a great teacher who has already achieved something remarkable, you can learn the secret to their success. You can then mirror what they have done, so that you can achieve similar success in your own life.

A great teacher or mentor will help you to stretch your realm of possibility. They will help you to overcome your self-imposed limitations. They will also help you to see what is really possible for you, and how up to that point, you have allowed yourself to put up with second best.

It's a bit like a small box that is placed inside a larger box. The small box represents what you believe to be possible for

"Textile king, shipping king, railroad king ... and a plain old King."

you right now. On the other hand, the larger box that surrounds it represents what is actually possible for you. The distance between the small box and the surrounding outer box represents how much you need to stretch your life in order to achieve your true potential.

Likewise, a mentor will challenge you, forcing you to expand your life and overcome your limitations, and they will show you through their own example what is actually possible for you.

A mentor can be a highly experienced person who you meet with from time to time, who you can ask questions of and get guidance from on the specific subject are you trying to master.

On the other hand, your mentor could simply be a well-known author you learn from, but never actually meet in person. Obviously, you could get more benefit if you are able to reach out to your mentor from time to time to get their advice. However, you can still learn an enormous amount just from their books, courses, and seminars.

Coaching Gets You Even Faster Results

A personal coach is similar to a mentor, but they are someone who you interact with frequently and who gives you a more structured approach to achieving your goals. Just like with a mentor, they can help you to recognise and overcome your current limitations more easily. However, with coaching, you often have a greater chance of success, because their specific purpose is to help you achieve your goals as quickly as possible.

Your coach can help you to make changes that will improve every area of your life. A coach may or may not have the exact skillset that you wish to master, but they will help keep you accountable and moving forwards, rather than regressing and giving up. By seeking out and finding a great coach, you will be giving yourself the greatest gift you can ever reward yourself with.

When you start working with a coach, they will ask you about the things that you wish to achieve in your life, and what you feel may be holding you back the most. They will then create a plan that will help you to achieve those goals. A coach is not just an accountability partner; coaching goes far further than that. By using a coach, you will be committing yourself to a far better life. Coaching is fun, but it is also a very serious business, because it can bring you tangible, measurable results very fast.

Many people who set serious goals for themselves often work alone. They rely on their own existing resources, knowledge, and understanding. This can work well if they are already disciplined, very knowledgeable, deeply resourceful, and persistent.

However, most people **The results** require the assistance of **bear** another experienced person **me out** in order to achieve really big goals. Your coach will help you keep on track, see potential in yourself that you did not know you possessed, act as a sounding board, give you feedback and validation, as well as empower you to break through every obstacle in your path.

Almost all coaches have a coach themselves, because they understand how vital coaching is to their own success, and to the success of their clients. I have benefited greatly from my own personal coach. Coaching has helped me brainstorm new business ideas, and my coach has shared with me his vast experience in marketing, critiqued my writing, helped me to see where I was holding myself back, and he has been totally honest and truthful in his feedback.

My coach has also provided me with some of the best training materials for subjects that I needed to master more deeply.

I'm also a member of a group coaching program with one of the world's best-known internet marketers and copywriters. Every two weeks, I attend a group coaching call with a well-known business celebrity.

Here, I can ask questions, get my marketing materials reviewed, and learn the most up-to-date and most effective marketing methods that are working well right now. These group coaching calls have enabled me to understand and implement complex marketing strategies and campaigns quickly and easily — campaigns that without this coaching, I would have never even attempted!

My Own Coaching Programs

I myself am a coach and provide my one-on-one clients with Certified High Performance Coaching. This is an advanced level of coaching that allows you to succeed above and beyond standard norms consistently over the long-term. It is available to clients who have already achieved some level of success in their life, and it goes far beyond what most coaching programs can ever achieve. At the time of publication of this book, it has achieved an amazing 94% satisfaction rating in 30,000 coaching sessions, which is far above life-coaching industry norms.

I also run a group coaching program named Ultimate Success Club that is open to anyone who is serious about achieving their goals. You can find out more details about both coaching programs, and avail of a very special offer for readers of this book at:

www.mikepettigrew.com/special/

Mentors and Coaches Guarantee Your Success

I cannot overemphasise the importance of mentors and coaches. Whatever it is you wish to achieve, please seek out outstanding teachers, and put into practice what you learn. You may need several mentors, each covering a different area, depending on the goals you wish to achieve. I have several world-class mentors to whom I am deeply grateful. Mentors who have enabled me to achieve far more in a single year than I would have in a decade on my own through trial and error.

Then, if you want to totally transform your life and increase your chances of success 100-fold, please give yourself the gift of working with a coach. Quickly, you may discover that it was the very best investment you have ever made in your life.

Coaching can improve all areas of your life, and its effects on your family can be truly dramatic, allowing you to be a better partner to your spouse, and better parent to your children.

How to Find and Contact a Mentor or Coach

Today finding a mentor or coach is not difficult, as there are many people who can assist you, such as well-known authors and trainers.

Here are just a few ways that can help you to seek out and contact your own mentor or coach:

> ➤ Choose what you want to learn
> ➤ Seek out mentors and coaches — bestselling authors on Amazon are a great place to start
> ➤ Read their books and do their courses
> ➤ If they already have a mentoring or coaching program, join it!
> ➤ If not, write out your expectations for personal mentoring/coaching
> ➤ Contact them by email or phone asking whether they would consider mentoring/coaching you

Mastermind Groups

Many years ago, when I read *Think and Grow Rich* for the first time, I came across the concept of mastermind groups. Napoleon Hill had interviewed hundreds of the world's most successful people, and he discovered that most of them had access to a specialised group of individuals, which he called a <u>mastermind group</u>. Each of these highly successful people use their own mastermind group to brainstorm new ideas, and to find solutions to existing problems.

When any group of experienced people come together, they can come up with creative solutions to problems more quickly and easily than if they had acted alone.

For example, Henry Ford, the creator of the first automobiles, used his mastermind group in all sorts of ways. Ford had very little schooling, and there were many gaps in his education. However, he was able to bridge those knowledge gaps by drawing on the resources of his mastermind group. His group was made up of mathematicians, engineers, and scientific minds, and it enabled him to progress his goals far more quickly. If there was ever a problem he needed to solve, he would meet his mastermind group and discuss it with them. This allowed him to quickly overcome problems and bring his ideas to fruition much faster.

I too have my own mastermind group, and I have found it to be an invaluable resource. Every two weeks, I get together with two other people who also run their own successful businesses. We have our meetings using online video conferencing. I am based in Ireland, while my two colleagues are located in Slovakia, and on the West Coast of the United States.

During each mastermind session, we speak for an hour or two. We are all experts in business and marketing, and we share with each other experiments we are conducting and the results of those experiments. We also help each other learn new skills, and fill in the gaps in each other's knowledge when needed.

It's remarkable how much we have helped each other's businesses. Our conversations are fun, educational, and extremely rewarding. I am certain that you too could benefit from a mastermind group.

Your Own Mastermind Group

When you get together regularly with a small group of people who are also serious about progressing their goals, it can benefit you all enormously. However, if you are all beginners, you need to be careful that you do not burden each other with your own doubts and previous failures.

Many mastermind groups are made up of people who are in the same field of business, but this is not essential. A mastermind group

**"He had an uncanny ability
to pick up the scent of opportunity."**

that is made up of people in different types of business, but who are all trying to grow their business, can be richly rewarding. If you all have exactly the same skills, the benefits may not be so great.

On the other hand, when each member of the group has some skills that the other members don't possess, then your interactions can be very powerful, and can help the group to an even greater extent.

One thing you will notice from your own mastermind group is that it motivates you to take action more quickly. You probably won't want to be the only one who hasn't made any progress in their projects! This is a great way of keeping each of you accountable and moving forwards. You will also find that it renews your vitality and enthusiasm for each of your projects.

What you will learn from each member of your group will be enormous, and it will affect what you do and what you focus on the most.

I wanted to be part of a mastermind group for many years, but each time I was considering creating one, the potential members did not have sufficient experience. In such cases, had I moved forwards, I would have ended up being a teacher, instead of also benefiting from the group. If you are already very experienced in your own particular mastermind topic and the other members are not, then bear this in mind. Otherwise, you could just end up being a mentor to everyone in your group! You must all benefit from the group if it's to work the most effectively.

Today, my own group consists of three businesspeople with a lot of experience, and that's why our group works so well. So, please don't rush to get people in your group. Rather, be very selective, and realise that each person in your group should have something valuable to contribute in order for the group to work effectively and benefit everyone. Otherwise, your mastermind group could fade out quite quickly, as people won't get much benefit from it and will start to lose interest.

Creating the "right" mastermind group can help you in many ways, including keeping you moving forwards and allowing you to achieve your goals more quickly.

How to Create a Mastermind Group

When you seek out and form a group of people who all have a common purpose, it can benefit every member of that group enormously. Ideally, you want at least one person in that group to have more experience than you have.

You could even create a mastermind group of people who all have more experience than you by being the person who brings the highly-experienced people together. They will all really appreciate you for doing this, and you could learn and gain far more than you would from people who are all at the same experience level as you.

Ideally, you can create the group for up to 6 people (possibly competitors) who are all in the same field of business in which you want to gain more understanding. If you mention to each of them the names of the other people who you intend to add to the group, it could strongly motivate them to join your group.

Meeting Frequency:

Your mastermind group could meet weekly or every two weeks, depending on the needs and priorities of the members. Every member of your mastermind group will have different experiences and perspectives that can benefit the entire group. However, it's important to have some sort of agenda, so that each member of the group can share a success story and also mention the things that they need help with from other group members.

It's also best to have a time-keeper and this responsibility can be rotated among each member if necessary. It's important to be strict with time-keeping, because some people may always try to hog the sessions and others may not get their needs met. Should this start happening, the mastermind group could begin to fall apart. Therefore, to avoid this scenario as far as possible, it's advisable to nominate a time-keeper who keeps an eye on the time to ensure that everybody in the group gets their needs met.

Your mastermind group can also help its members stay accountable for achieving their goals. It could be worthwhile to get each member to commit to progressing one or more of their goals in some way by the next mastermind session. Then during the next meeting, you can review whether or not they achieved it, or whether a course adjustment is needed.

It may appear like a daunting task to call up competitors and invite them to join your mastermind group — especially if they have a lot more experience and far more success than you currently have. You may be completely new to the industry and feel very inadequate and inexperienced. However, most likely they will all really appreciate you for doing this, because it allows each of them to discover what's working best in their industry and enables them to learn from other highly successful people.

In fact, they may even be worried that if they don't join your mastermind group, they could miss out on an important industry peer group that could help them and their business in a very substantial way!

Here is a sample telephone script that you could use when cold-calling prospective members for your mastermind group. You could also modify it, so that its suitable for e-mail.

Sample Script for Getting Mastermind Group Members

Hi, [NAME].

My name is [YOUR NAME], and I'm a [BUSINESS TYPE] and I [VERY BRIEF DESCRIPTION OF WHAT YOU DO IN YOUR BUSINESS].

I've got some interest from a number of people who want to form a mastermind group of the top people in our industry.

This group will help all of us to gain access to new solutions, resources, and perspectives that we had probably never thought of before.

I really wanted you to be part of this special group, because I believe you will get a lot of value from it. Unless of course, you are already part of such a mastermind group? [WAIT FOR RESPONSE].

Can I put you on our list? The group will meet [BY PHONE/SKYPE/IN PERSON ETC – choose whatever mode is most appropriate for your group] every [week / every 2 weeks] to brainstorm new ideas and help each other with any challenges we may be facing.

It will mean that you can benefit from the insight and perspectives of those who are also at the top of our field, and discover new ideas for growing your business that you may never have even thought of.

Note:

At this point, if you can name-drop an industry leader who has already decided to join your group (or who is considering joining it), it could be a massive motivator for them to agree to join!

Creating your own mastermind group (or joining an existing one) could be one of the biggest actions you can ever take to move yourself to the next level of success. And it could even mean that you quickly "jump up several levels" of that ladder.

A mastermind group really can be powerful at turning your creative ideas into concrete, tangible results that magnify your success ten-fold.

Summary:

➤ **Lifelong education is vitally important** — Robotics and artificial intelligence is changing the world. You must learn new skills and become more capable from now on.

➤ **Success can be learned** — There is no need to reinvent the wheel. Seek out excellent teachers and you can succeed at anything you want.

➤ **Transform your life** — Mentors and coaches will help you overcome your current limitations, learn new skills, and achieve your goals more quickly.

➤ **Coaching for success** — A good coach is the greatest gift you can ever give yourself. Coaching is one of the fastest and easiest ways to ensure you achieve your goals.

➤ **Mastermind groups** — A group of people with a common purpose is powerful. You can brainstorm, learn new skills, keep yourself accountable, and always moving forwards.

Magnifier: Your True Purpose

Everyone needs a sense of purpose – a belief that what they are doing is important, and that it makes a difference in the world around them. Making the effort to find your own unique purpose in life could be one of the most important actions you make during your lifetime.

Living your life with a sense of deep purpose and commitment is a source of great joy and fulfilment. It is also a source of incredible power — transforming your life and making what once seemed impossible into something that's very achievable.

Gandhi, Einstein, Edison, Bill Gates, Steve Jobs, and others transformed the world with their ideas and their creations. What made these people great and allowed them to achieve incredible goals in the face of seemingly insurmountable obstacles was their strong belief and their keen sense of purpose.

Likewise, when you find a deeper purpose in your own life, you can truly achieve anything you desire and your life will never be the same again.

Near Death Experiences

I started my own journey to discover my life's purpose a long time ago. I was only 15 years old at the time, and my life had just changed completely. It was a beautiful sunny day with a cloudless blue sky, as I walked to my Dad's church with my mother. It was one of those days when it feels truly great to be alive.

As I walked up the road, I felt excited and elated, rather than the emotions you might expect when you've just lost your favourite cousin. Peter was my hero, and I was closer to him than any of my other cousins. He was a few years older than me, and he had just started university. One day, while cycling his bicycle, Peter was struck by a car, and later died in hospital.

My family was totally devastated. It was hard to believe that someone who had been so full of life could leave this world so quickly. The shock was enormous, and I'll never forget it. However, the day of Peter's funeral seemed more like a celebration than the deep loss it really was. At the time, I didn't understand why I seemed to feel more alive that day than I ever had before. It's like I had been given a gift, rather than losing someone who I had been very close to.

Some months later, my aunt and uncle gave me a book that totally changed my life. The name of that book was *Life After Life* by Dr Raymond Moody. This amazing book was the first of its kind, and it contained many first-hand reports of near death experiences. Dr Moody interviewed many people who had clinically died, but who were eventually resuscitated.

In some cases, the patient would have no recollections of what had happened during the time they were clinically dead. However, Raymond Moody was also told by many of these patients how they had found themselves floating above their physical body, as the doctors and nurses tried to resuscitate on them.

In many cases, these people who were clinically dead, moved through walls, and overheard conversations that were later verified as having actually taken place. Others found themselves moving through a tunnel, and entering a realm that was completely different from physical reality.

Many of these people reported having been reunited with deceased relatives and loved ones, and in many cases undergoing a life review, in the presence of a being of light. At this point, people would usually interpret this being of light according to their religious beliefs and traditions.

Some people claimed that this being of light was Jesus, Krishna, Mohammed, Buddha, a variety of other religious teachers, or a spirit guide.

However, further research has revealed that this being of light may in fact be our own higher self — the part of us that is connected to universal life itself.

This being of light often shows the individual a life review. Or rather, the individual starts experiencing everything they have ever done in life, from the moment they were born right up to the point where they died. This life review

"I'm your Guardian Angel, but I choose to let you handle this yorself."

contains the full emotional impact of the original experiences, and all the senses are involved.

The person going through this experience literally relives every experience of their life, but not just from their own personal perspective. Many people have reported that they also feel the effects of their actions on others too. They experience the love that they have given others, as well as the suffering and pain that they have caused during their life.

In effect, this life review is an opportunity for the person to assess the life they have lived, and evaluate their own actions and reactions. Most people who have experienced this are very clear about what it entails. Rather than the being of light judging them, they instead act as a friendly counsel.

Since this ground-breaking book was released, millions of people have come forward with similar experiences, and many of them insist that we are not judged after death. Rather, it is we who judge ourselves. During the life review stage of a near death experience, people who have caused a lot of suffering to others feel great remorse for the pain that they have created. They also feel great joy for the love and acts of kindness that they have made towards others.

As you will discover, near death experiences can tell us a lot about the purpose of life and what we "should" be doing while we are alive, but there are many people who are sceptical about the reality of this phenomenon. However, there is clear evidence that shows such experiences are not the product of one's imagination.

Real-World Correlation

Millions of people have had near death experiences, and most of them cannot be attributed to such things as oxygen deprivation, or trauma induced hallucinations. When near death experiencers overhear conversations and witness events that are physically distant from their dead physical body, something very real must be happening. This is because their perceptions of distant events that occurred while they were no longer limited to their physical senses can often be verified later.

Likewise, many people who have had a near death experience had information communicated to them by deceased friends and relatives that is later verified as being correct — knowledge and information that they did not have access to prior to their own temporary physical death. This real-world validation shows us that near death experiences are not products of the imagination, or fantasies brought on by a brain that is in the early stages of death.

Since 1975, a great deal of research has been conducted in the field of life after physical death. This includes many scientific studies by well-known doctors and cardiologists who have staked their entire reputation on their findings. My own great journey into this research began when I was only 15 years old. Since then, I have spent the past 40 years studying the nature of human consciousness and the mind. Being a sceptic, I like to dig deep – very deep.

Since I'm very scientifically-minded, I like to see, touch, and feel as much evidence as possible before accepting anything that could simply be dismissed as an illusion. In my research over many years, I have found that in the arena of life after death studies, there seems to be a lot of significant misinformation, due in part to the New Age movement. New Age is simply a melting pot of all sorts of ideas, many of which are conflicting. Much of New Age thought appears to be solid, while at the same time, there is much that should to be questioned a lot more deeply to uncover the truth.

The subject of life after death fascinates me, and I know from my own experiences that when we finally understand why we are here, it can affect everything we do from that point forwards. It can give our entire life deeper meaning and purpose.

At this point, it would be very easy to think that what I have said is just my own personal views, but I assure you that it is not. When you take the time to research the evidence for life after death in detail yourself, I'm pretty sure you will discover these very same truths for yourself. And there are many ways to explore the evidence for life after death, and to discover the purpose of physical life. These include the study of near death experiences, hypnotic regression into past lives, the use of technology to expand awareness and consciousness, as well as other areas of research.

The scientific method is based on repeatable results, and repeatable findings. Whenever large numbers of researchers discover exactly the same things, powerful elements of truth are being uncovered.

For further reading, you could explore the research and studies by:

➤ Cardiologist Pim van Lommel
➤ Dr Sam Parnia
➤ Dr Raymond Moody
➤ Professor Ian Stevenson
➤ Dr Brian L Weiss
➤ Robert Monroe and the Monroe Institute

Life's True Purpose

The subject of death is one that frightens a lot of people, and most people avoid this subject like the plague. Often, it's much later in life that we start to ask the really big questions like *why am I here, what should I be doing, and what will happen to me after I die?*

A 13th century sage once said, *"first of all learn about death, and then about other things"*. He said this over 700 years ago, at a time when

"I want to tap into my higher self."

learning about death was extremely difficult to do. However, we now live in an age when we know more about our world, the universe, and our place in it than at any other time in human history.

We live in an age when there is an explosion of knowledge and understanding available to us right now. And, by taking the time to study this fascinating subject in depth, it can totally change your understanding about your own life.

Digging deep while remaining sceptical, and sifting through the more questionable "evidence", you will most likely discover that the life you are living right now is more important than you may ever have imagined. And what you are doing while you are alive has very big effects on those around you, as well as your own spiritual essence.

Please don't get me wrong, I am not talking about religion here. Unfortunately, religion is responsible for many of the world's problems today. I'm not saying that religion is bad, but it has been misinterpreted and used as an excuse for all sorts of atrocities, and it has been used this way for centuries. The fact is, these days people need a lot more than just blind faith – they need evidence and when they get that evidence, real understanding can emerge.

Most people who have near death experiences become deeply spiritual as a result, with an insatiable curiosity about life, and in many cases, they stop practising organised religion. However, they do realise that the core of most religious traditions are correct. They discover that the most important thing they can do as a human being is to <u>become wiser, more compassionate, more courageous, and contribute more to the happiness of those around them.</u>

A Shared Common Purpose

According to the findings of thousands of researchers around the world, we all share a very similar purpose. **We are here in this world to grow spiritually, and help others in any way that we can.** Again, when I say "spiritually" I'm not referring to religion. To grow spiritually means to develop our inner qualities, and use those qualities to help enrich the lives of others.

However, to grow spiritually often means that we must experience some level of suffering. It's a bit like polishing a diamond. We need to cut off the rough edges for the sparkling diamond to emerge. All the challenges we experience in life, all of the heartache, suffering, and pain seems to be designed to help us to grow. It's almost like these experiences are tailor-made for our growth.

However, there is a limit to the amount of suffering that is valuable for our growth. Sadly, it's possible to get "locked" into a continual loop of negative thoughts and emotions and to sink into pessimism. There always comes a point where we need to choose the way we want to be, rather than allowing our suffering to perpetuate.

Unfortunately, without difficulty, people generally do not change. Without suffering, we would not be as motivated to help others. Without experiencing loss, we would have no resources to help other people to transform their similar circumstances. This is the reason why I do what I do.

During my life, I have discovered a lot of very tangible evidence for life after death. I have also experienced many big hardships along the way. I feel that it is a crime to go through life and discover truths that can really help people, and not share those truths with others, in a way that can truly benefit them.

Likewise, I believe that every painful experience we go through in life should be used to help others overcome similar situations. If we are not using our own past experiences in some way to also help others, then we may not be fulfilling one of our bigger purposes in life.

A Deeper Purpose

Earlier in this book, I explained how important it is to uncover your own deep purpose for each of your goals. When you attach each of your goals to a greater purpose, then it can speed up the attainment of that goal.

However, we can go even further with this. By truly understanding that your purpose as a human being is to learn all that you can, experience as much of life as possible, and make a difference in the lives of other people, you will ultimately be motivated to start living your life more creatively and possibly even more responsibly.

So, whenever you create any big goal, it may be very beneficial to ask yourself — *can what you are setting out to achieve also benefit others in a tangible way? Also, will your goal help you to grow in ways that can enhance your mission as a human being, and is it truly the best use of your time?*

Your Own Unique Purpose

Although it seems that as human beings we all share a common purpose, everybody also needs a strong individual purpose (or purposes) to be truly happy and fulfilled. We all need to feel like we make some sort of difference, and if we are denied this, then we can end up feeling frustrated and powerless.

I honestly believe that a life without direction or purpose can often be a sad, unfulfilling one, where very little is achieved or accomplished. On the other hand, when you start to live your life with deeper meaning and purpose, then everything becomes possible for you. Your journey will become every bit as thrilling as your destination, and you will start to experience what it truly means to be alive.

The fact is, unless we feel that we are contributing to something greater than ourselves, then life can become meaningless and monotonous. And, no matter how successful you may become, unless you feel a sense of deep purpose, your success may not make you feel any different than before.

It's very possible to become rich and successful and feel very empty inside. There is no point trying to achieve anything, unless when you achieve it — the effects enhance your overall happiness and wellbeing. The world has far too many "successful people" who are deeply unhappy.

On the other hand, when you connect your goals to a purpose that is worthwhile and that contributes to others in a significant way, then even the journey itself can be a source of deep happiness and enrichment for you.

No two people are exactly alike, and we all have a unique make up. You have within you right now all sorts of strengths, abilities, interests, and passions that make you who you are. And you have also developed all sorts of resources within yourself, through your own life experiences.

At some point in your life, it's important to become consciously aware of your own unique mission in life. The things that you absolutely love doing — that can also help other people. When you become aware of such a purpose, it can have a very big impact on your overall long-term happiness level.

Now I'm not necessarily talking about anything grandiose here, but rather your own unique contributions to the world around you. In fact, research into near death experiences suggest that it is the small spontaneous acts of kindness that we make during our life that matter most.

But if we can combine fulfilling our mission as a human being (growing spiritually and helping others in any way that we can) with the unique skills that we possess, then we can act as a powerful catalyst for change in the lives of others. So how can you find your own unique major life purpose?

Your Passions and Your Major Life Purpose (MLP)

Confucius once said, *"Choose a job you love, and you will never have to work a day in your life."* This means that when you start doing what you love, your life will become enriched in every way.

Sadly, many people get trapped in jobs that they hate, and they can see no real way out. However, even if where you are right now is not where you want to be at all, then by starting to carry out your <u>major life purpose</u> (MLP) right now, you "qualify" yourself for the next stepping stone to success, and to fulfilling your mission in a far greater way.

Many people struggle with this because they are trying to find "that **one** thing" or purpose that they were "born to do". However, this can be the very reason why they feel like something is missing from their life. The idea that each of us has only one thing that we are meant to do can limit us greatly from fulfilling our greatness as human beings.

"I'm about to achieve one of the greatest passions of my life: dessert."

Every human being is simply too complex to be limited to only one single activity.

So rather than limiting yourself to finding your "one unique purpose" in life, it's far easier to start getting in touch with your passions! This is because when you start leading a passionate life, then you also start living your life with greater purpose.

When you do this, the feeling that something is missing will start to go away. The real need to seek "our purpose" often comes from a lack of passion, because when you don't feel connected to your life, you lack purpose and passion.

The important thing is to actually *decide* what you "mission" will be, instead of aimlessly searching for it. Then the process of finding your MLP is not as difficult as it may first appear.

Passion + Daily Action = MLP

When you are passionate about certain things in your life, and you take consistent actions in those areas, then you start living your life with far greater purpose. Although you may discover that you do have a "single" overall MLP, you will also find that you have several passions or avenues through which you can express that purpose.

For example, my own MLP is "to inspire, motivate, and empower people, so they can achieve their goals, and become deeply happy". I also have several avenues through which I express that purpose. For example, as a husband, a father, an author, a coach, and an entrepreneur. These are the avenues or passions that I use to fulfil my overall MLP.

So, to discover your own MLP, all you need to do is start exploring your passions! As you gradually become clearer about what your purpose is, then write it out in the form of a concise empowering statement.

However, please be aware that this may not be something you can simply do overnight. It could take introspection and careful analysis before you can produce it in its final form.

It may even take several weeks before you come up with a concise MLP that feels exactly right, and that is a true expression of your innermost values and directions. Later, you may wish to review it from time to time and make minor changes to it as your life progresses.

Here are some of the MLP statements of several famous people, and also the mission statements of well-known companies that may give you some food for thought:

> *"To make a significant difference in the quality of life of people."*
> – Anthony Robbins

> *"I shall not submit to injustice from anyone. I shall conquer untruth by truth."*
> – Mahatma Gandhi

> *"To be a teacher. And to be known for inspiring my students to be more than they thought they could be."*
> – Oprah Winfrey

> *"To have fun in (my) journey through life and learn from (my) mistakes."*
> - Richard Branson

> *"To Unite People & Promote Equality."*
> – Martin Luther King

> *"To serve as a leader, live a balanced life, and apply ethical principles to make a significant difference."*
> – Denise Morrison, Campbell Soup Company

> *"To contribute to the making of a just society... a democratic and free society in which all persons live together in harmony and with equal opportunities."*
> – Nelson Mandela

"To elevate the financial wellbeing of our clients."
— Robert Kiyosaki

"It's our goal to be Earth's most customer-centric company, where customers can find and discover anything they might want to buy online."
— Amazon

"Facebook's mission is to give people the power to share and make the world more open and connected."
— Facebook

"To inspire and nurture the human spirit - one person, one cup and one neighbourhood at a time."
- Starbucks

Do This Exercise: How to Discover Your MLP

So how can you discover your own MLP and the main avenues through which you can express it? Here is a simple technique that will help you to find your MLP:

STEP 1: Brainstorm your unique contributions to the world so far. Also, make a list of your current skills, as well as those things that give you most enjoyment in life.

The following are just some questions you can ask yourself to narrow down on your MLP:

> What activities make you feel most alive?
> If you knew you could not fail, what would you love to do?
> If you were a billionaire, what would you spend your time doing?
> What do you enjoy learning about most?
> What issues have been a constant theme throughout your life?
> What do you enjoy talking about most with others?
> What kind of giving is most rewarding for you?
> What have you struggled with most throughout your life?
> What are your most unique talents that you excel in?

STEP 2: Start writing out possibilities of what your unique contributions might be — the things that make you feel most alive and that could help other people.

STEP 3: Don't stop until you run out of ideas! The right idea will most likely give you a huge sense of excitement when you write it out.

STEP 4: Now complete your MLP sentence: "My unique contribution to the world is to_____

_____"

Here is a process chart to clarify the exercise:

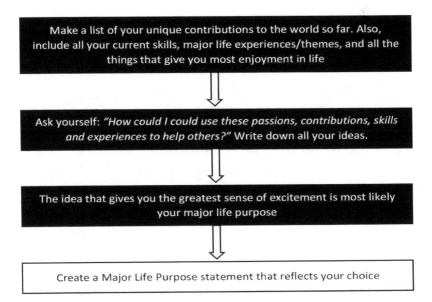

Make a list of your unique contributions to the world so far. Also, include all your current skills, major life experiences/themes, and all the things that give you most enjoyment in life

Ask yourself: *"How could I could use these passions, contributions, skills and experiences to help others?"* Write down all your ideas.

The idea that gives you the greatest sense of excitement is most likely your major life purpose

Create a Major Life Purpose statement that reflects your choice

You now need to commit to your MLP, and start taking actions to achieve it. To do this, modify your existing action plans, and/or create new ones — taking into consideration this MLP you have created.

If you are having any difficulty doing this exercise, or finding it hard to come up with ideas that feel just right, then try using the creative inner genius technique I will share with you in the next chapter. Use it to get your subconscious mind to help you become aware of what activities you should be doing to enable you to live a happy, fulfilling, creative life.

The True Value of Your Time

Few people truly understand how valuable their time actually is. When you are focused and highly motivated, you can progress a goal more quickly in a single day than you may normally do in a month, or even a year. Your time is the most valuable thing you possess — time gives you unlimited potential. You can use it in any way you choose, or you can waste it in every way imaginable.

If you want to understand just how valuable your time is, spend a few days as a volunteer in a hospice. Hospice patients are at the very end of their physical life, and yet they can experience inner changes that can appear like miracles.

For several years, I worked as a volunteer in a hospice, spending my time with people who were very close to the end of their life. People who are dying usually realise they have very little time left to change painful family relationships. However, most people think that they can put off until a later point changes they know they should be making right now. For example, painful relationships, disagreements, or family feuds.

However, when faced with the reality that time has almost run out, people can address and overcome lifetimes of baggage - often in a single day. When you realise that you can no longer put off healing a wound with a family member, all sorts of things become possible.

The fact is, we don't know when our time is up. It could be 40 or 50 years in the future, or it could even be tomorrow. On the other hand, **you need to start living today as though each day were your last day**. When you do so, you can accomplish anything, and make incredible progress in all that you do. Your time is the most precious commodity that you possess in your life. And how you use your time and energy is very important.

When you reach the end of your life, do you want to be able to look back and say to yourself that you gave it your all, you did your very best, and that you regret nothing? Or will you leave this life filled with regrets and wishing that you had done more for those around you? To truly live a life of no regrets, you need to apply yourself with passion and enthusiasm to everything that you do, while working towards your goals consistently.

You also need to consider taking actions to empower other people to the best of your ability. When you do this, you become a "beacon of light" for others and a source of hope and strength. Surely, this is the noblest way you can possibly live your life? When you start living this way, you will also be far more powerfully connected to your inner wisdom, your source of empowerment and abundant life force. You will connect into a limitless source of energy that will help you to transform your goals into reality, and far more quickly.

There is an intriguing saying, "giving all is gaining all". This is so true, because when we develop a life of greater contribution, it really is us who gain the most. Just like I explained earlier, gratitude acts like a magnet – drawing into your life all sorts of amazing benefits, and unlocking all sorts of possibilities that would never have been available to you.

Likewise, when you are outward-looking and you make efforts to help other people in a long-term sustained way, then it can help transform every area of your own life too. It's just like pulling the corner of a spider's web — the entire web changes shape. Taking actions for the happiness of others will help you to achieve the happiest life possible, and allow you to achieve your goals far more quickly.

It's important to mention here that I am definitely not suggesting you start to practice the art of self-sacrifice! Self-sacrifice is never valuable, because it often leads to diminishing one's own self-worth, which is the opposite to what you need to achieve. Your own needs are extremely important, but so are the needs of others. And if you are running around helping everybody with their problems but ignoring your own, then it could be a sign that you are avoiding something painful.

It's easy to avoid facing some emotional issue when you spend all your time helping others — but avoidance will cost you greatly in the long run. Therefore, finding the best balance between fulfilling your own dreams and working for the happiness of others is important, and only you can truly determine what that balance is.

Summary:

➤ **Purpose** — Living with a sense of deep purpose is a source of joy and fulfilment. It allows you to achieve what once seemed impossible. Your purpose is your source of power.

➤ **A common purpose** — According to research into the evidence for life after death, we all share a common purpose: to grow and also help others to do the same.

➤ **Your own unique purpose** — You also have a unique purpose that can energise you. You can find this when you explore your passions, life experience, and talents.

➤ **Your time is valuable** — It's actually the most valuable thing you possess, and gives you unlimited potential to achieve anything you want. *Never waste time!*

Magnifier: Your Inner Genius

Your subconscious mind is not only responsible for the automated processes of your body, but also for the thoughts that you think and the beliefs that you carry deep within you.

"We call out to you, please reveal yourself, oh Spirit of Innovation."

There is also another fascinating aspect to your subconscious mind that is truly surprising and deeply empowering.

Your subconscious mind appears to act like a conduit to universal wisdom. It is a connecting link to unlimited wisdom that all human beings can access — when they know how.

As Napoleon Hill says in *Think and Grow Rich*:

> *"There is plenty of evidence to support the belief that the subconscious mind is the connecting link between the finite mind of man and Infinite Intelligence. It is the intermediary through which one may draw upon the forces of Infinite Intelligence at will. It, alone, contains the secret process by which mental impulses are modified and changed into their spiritual equivalent. It, alone, is the medium through which prayer may be transmitted to the source capable of answering prayer."*

There are numerous effective ways of connecting to this universal wisdom that lies deep in the mind of every human being. And it appears to be a source of wisdom that may even be outside the confines of your own life and physicality. In this chapter, you will learn how to connect with your inner wisdom and creativity, and use it to get answers to any problem, and also to enrich your life.

How to Get Answers to Any Problem

Many of the world's greatest scientists and inventors have been aware of this capability to get the answers to any problem, and they have used it to bring into the world amazing new technologies, inventions, and scientific discoveries.

A famous example of this was Thomas Edison, who used to take catnaps whenever he was stumped by a technical problem that he couldn't figure out with his conscious mind. Edison was the inventor of the incandescent light bulb, and many other inventions we use to this day, and whenever he was facing a problem to which he could not find a solution, he used to take a short nap for 30 to 60 minutes.

Before falling asleep, he would firmly plant into his mind the problem he needed a solution to, while fully expecting an answer to that problem. On awakening, he would often have the exact solution that he needed to solve his problem. It's almost like his subconscious mind would download into his conscious mind the solution that he needed.

You too can use the exact same technique, and you may be very surprised by the deep wisdom that you can access within your own mind. I have had many experiences of this myself, and I would like to share with you just one of these, so you can see how easy it is to access this wisdom and find solutions to any difficulties you may be facing in life.

A few years ago, I was facing a potentially serious business problem and I tried to figure out a solution to it in every way imaginable. I even hired experts to find a workable solution to the situation. If no solution were possible, then it would mean that I would lose hundreds of dollars each day. It was a pretty serious issue and I really needed to find a resolution as quickly as possible.

Unfortunately, neither of the two experts that I hired were able to find a workable way forwards, and I was deeply concerned, because our loss of profits was becoming quite a serious issue. I know it sounds crazy, but it took me some time before I remembered to hand this problem

"I found the door to the Land of Great Ideas."

over to my own mind to find a solution.

Eventually, I remembered what Thomas Edison used to do when confronted with similar issues. So one night before falling asleep, I focused on the problem and asked my inner wisdom to give me a solution upon awakening. I also worked myself into a state of truly believing that I would receive a solution to the problem the very next morning.

I then fell asleep only to awaken 30 minutes later. Amazingly, in my mind was the exact solution that I needed. It was literally downloaded into my mind as I woke up.

The next day, I contacted the experts I had hired and asked them whether the solution I had "discovered" would work and was safe to move forwards with. I was delighted to find that I had found a completely workable solution to the problem that the two independent experts themselves had never even considered. And it was a solution that would benefit my business in several other ways that I couldn't even have imagined.

Do This Exercise: Find Answers While You Sleep

The next time you are stumped by a problem that you can't seem to find a solution for, try this simple exercise.

Step 1: Think about the problem for a few minutes and how important it is that you find a solution to it fast.

Step 2: Tell yourself that you need a solution to the problem, and firmly state that you expect your inner genius to give you a solution upon awakening.

Step 3: Next, clearly visualise yourself wakening up the next morning, very excited that you now have a perfect solution to the problem. While doing this, trigger your GA so your visualisation is emotionalised.

Step 4: Finally, put any thoughts about the problem to one side and go to sleep.

Step 5: Your solution may present itself to you on awakening, or over the next few days in ways you may not have expected. If necessary, repeat this process until you discover a solution.

The important thing here is to be crystal clear on what you want, and to **expect an answer**. It's almost like you need to work up a feeling of total trust, or faith that you *will* receive a solution to your problem. Your subconscious mind can present the solution to you in various ways – your answer could come upon awakening, or sometime over the next few days.

Make sure you test this technique for yourself the next time you face a big problem where you just can't seem to find any solution. Although, do make sure you try it a bit quicker than I did! I really didn't have to go through such a long ordeal before finding an exciting, perfect solution within my own mind.

See the process chart on the next page:

Meditation is also an excellent way of connecting with this inner wisdom, and it's possible to move into this state quite quickly when you are proficient. There are very specific brain frequencies that are associated with meditative states, and whenever you successfully connect with this inner wisdom, it can be observed on an ordinary EEG machine that measures brain wave activity

Here is a process chart to clarify the exercise:

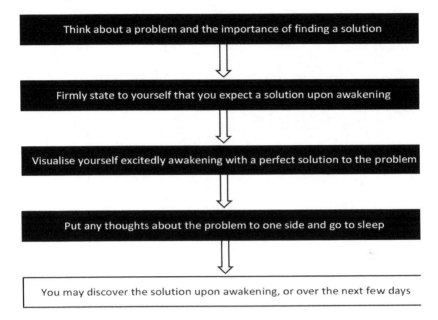

Think about a problem and the importance of finding a solution

Firmly state to yourself that you expect a solution upon awakening

Visualise yourself excitedly awakening with a perfect solution to the problem

Put any thoughts about the problem to one side and go to sleep

You may discover the solution upon awakening, or over the next few days

There are also several new technologies such as mind machines, which I have already shared with you, that can activate these same brain states even in people who have never had any prior experience of meditation.

Unlimited Creativity on Tap

Highly successful people understand that success, riches, and happiness are not created through hard work alone. Rather, these things are created by their ideas. You have within you a source of unlimited creative new ideas that can make you a fortune, and help you to achieve whatever you want in life.

You may already work very hard, yet still are not experiencing all the things you wish for. However, when you use your mind more creatively, you may be very surprised by what can happen.

Naturally, there are times when we are more creative, and also times where creativity seems to have vanished from our lives. However, it's possible to propel yourself out of any rut you may be experiencing when you start to exercise your "creativity muscles".

For example, we have all heard of "writer's block", and how many authors are prevented from writing by this apparently awful ailment.

But the truth is, it is possible to powerfully stimulate your creativity whenever you want. It's not even necessary to feel deeply inspired, or to wait for creativity to bestow its magical touch upon your mind before you can create a masterpiece.

Teacher's block.

There are powerful ways to stimulate your creativity, no matter how deep a rut you may find yourself in – you just need to take the right actions. You have within you right now a creative inner genius that you can tap into whenever you want, simply by starting to exercise your creativity muscles.

There have been many times in my own life when I have had to create something, but I have not felt in the least bit inspired to do so. However, when there has been an important need, I have been able to create my best work. So, you need to realise that **strong motivation always outweighs inspiration.**

Whenever we are motivated to create something unique, and start taking actions to create it, we find that the inspiration then comes naturally. It's almost like we need to **start stretching ourselves inside, before creativity can truly burst forth.**

Since your subconscious mind is connected to universal wisdom, which is unlimited, it is therefore possible for you to tap into this creativity whenever you need. Your mind and intentions are the connecting link, and it is completely your own responsibility whether you make that link successfully or not — all it takes is to get the process started. When you start stretching your creativity muscles, it can appear difficult at first, just like it is when we start exercising our physical muscles. But before long, creativity will start to burst forth from within you.

To stimulate your own inner creativity, you just need to get the process started — even if you feel completely uninspired and you don't feel at all creative. The act of *making efforts* to stimulate your creativity in and of itself opens the channel to your inner creative genius.

You have within you right now all sorts of extraordinarily creative ideas just waiting to get out. When you start tapping this creativity and applying it to different areas of your life, you may be astounded by what can happen.

If I asked you to come up with 10 ways that you could improve your health, would you be able to do so? I'm pretty sure you can easily come up with many ways to become healthier. For example, doing more exercise, getting more sleep, drinking more water, eating better-quality nutritious foods, getting more recreation and relaxation time, to name just a few possibilities.

Likewise, if I asked you to come up with 10 ideas for smartphone apps, would you be defeated? At first, particularly if you are not a "techie", you might find this challenge a lot more difficult. But after spending a couple of hours in one of the smartphone app stores, I'm sure you can "dream up" all sorts of ideas for new apps, or to improve existing ones.

Creativity "Muscle" Boosting Technique

To get your creativity muscles well and truly exercised so that you can greatly boost your ongoing creative potential, here is a useful exercise you can try for yourself, over the next week.

DAY 1: Write out a list of 10 things that you could do to express your gratitude to others. These should be things you can easily do that will show your appreciation to those who have helped you in some way.

DAY 2: Write out a list of 10 things that you could do to improve your physical health. These can be anything that you could do to become healthier.

DAY 3: Write down 10 ways you could improve your emotional health. These will be things that could contribute to your overall well-being and happiness.

It's also important to include some ideas that could help other people in meaningful ways too. This is because your own happiness is always directly connected to the efforts you also make towards the happiness of those around you.

DAY 4: We have all used apps on our smartphones and most of us have a good idea of what sort of apps are available in the app stores. So, your next exercise is to come up with 10 ideas for smartphone apps.

It doesn't matter if you later find that some of these apps already exist, but just start writing and see what happens. Some of your ideas may not be great at all, while others may surprise you. An app is something that makes people's lives better or easier or helps them in some way. So, go and look at the App Store on your phone to see what sort of apps people are creating. Then come up with 10 of your own ideas.

"I assume all this playing will lead to innovation."

DAY 5: Come up with 10 things you could do to bring more fun and excitement into your life. These should be things that you can start doing easily and put into practice right away.

Many of us move through each day almost on autopilot, simply reacting to what happens to us. But when we take stock of what we are currently doing and what we could be doing, it allows us to bring a lot more excitement and variety into our lives. These could be different ways in which you can reward yourself for all the efforts you are making to improve your life.

DAY 6: Write out a list of 10 things that you could do to simplify your life. Life can get very busy and you may be constantly running around trying to get everything done instead of looking for new ways that could save you time and energy.

There are all sorts of ways to make your life simpler without having to sacrifice your happiness or commitments to others. Think "minimum effort for the maximum result". When you save time and energy, the quality of your life improves, and you can have an even greater impact on the lives of others.

DAY 7: Write down a list of the three biggest problems in your life right now. Once you've done this, write down at least 3 things that you could do to overcome each one of those problems.

In these creativity exercises, you don't have to stop at 10 ideas. If ideas start to come tumbling out of you, then please keep going! 15 or 20 ideas is a lot better than just 10. Likewise, if you find it hard to come up with 10 creative ideas, then simply write down as many as you can within a reasonable time.

The more you do exercises like this, the more you will exercise your creativity muscles and you will develop a powerful creative resource that you can tap into whenever you need.

Keep an Ideas Notebook
At the end of just one week, you will probably be very surprised by your own ability to come up with creative ideas whenever you wish. By writing down your ideas for achieving your goals, and by doing this frequently, you will keep your creativity muscles exercised and in great shape.

This will allow you to tap into your creativity whenever you wish and use it to create all sorts of wonderful things in your life. Remember to keep a special notebook for all your new ideas and don't worry if some of them are nuts! Because when you do this, you will have plenty of great ideas too.

Never allow your internal editor to stop you – just keep the process flowing. What I mean by your internal editor is the part of you that tells you to delete the last sentence or the last idea because it isn't good enough. Simply let all your ideas flow without any restraint, and then after the process is completed, you can start editing if you really want to.

Whatever you wish to change or create in your life, everything starts with an idea. And the more great ideas you have, the easier it will be to improve your life and achieve your goals.

Here is one final thought on this subject for you to consider. If you were to spend just one hour each week coming up with new ideas to improve your life, and discovering ideas that could help you achieve your goals, how different do you think your life would be? So, add this creativity practice to your weekly schedule for at least one hour each week!

Summary:

➤ **Get answers to any problem** - Use the powerful exercise to get answers to any problem, directly from your subconscious mind.

➤ **Use the creativity muscle boosting technique** - Use this simple technique to ensure you always have a stream of great new ideas for achieving your goals.

➤ **Ideas notebook** - Write down all your new ideas in a special notebook, and keep it close to you at all times.

Bringing It All Together

At this point, I want to congratulate you for making it this far! So many people start a new book or course only to never complete it. This is very sad, because such people never manage to achieve their life's biggest goals and are doomed to a life of mediocrity and disillusionment.

On the other hand, the fact that you have made it this far proves that you are a winner and that you are a lot closer to achieving all your goals from now on. Well done!

In this book, you have discovered the Most Powerful Goal Achievement System in the World and why it is different and more effective than other goal achievement systems. You have in your hands a simple effective formula that cannot fail to bring you what you want — when you put it into practice.

At the beginning for this book, I made you a very big promise, and I want to make it again right here, right now. Providing you take action on what you have learned in this book, you can expect major positive transformations in your life.

If there is one great failing in human beings, it is learning something that can totally transform their lives, but never actually using it to create lasting change. Please do test this system fully for yourself, and don't just put this book on the self to gather dust — because, when you take action on what you have learned, your life will never be the same again.

In these pages, you have discovered:

➤ There are 7 exact steps that will allow you to achieve whatever you want, 10 times faster and easier.

➤ Goals can create major transformations in your life, and that it's easy to drift through life without setting them, or without keeping yourself accountable.

➤ Becoming very clear about what you want is not difficult, even if you were not quite sure to begin with.

➤ Your subconscious mind controls every area of your life, and you can use powerful mind programming tools to program your mind for success, and to create whatever you want.

➤ That your dominant thoughts, beliefs, emotions, actions, and reactions create the circumstances of your life.

➤ By changing these aspects, you can attract wonderful new experiences into your life and achieve your goals more easily.

➤ There is scientific evidence that validates this, and similar experiments that you can try for yourself.

➤ Your beliefs have the power to hold you back or to propel you forwards to achieve your goals more quickly.

➤ It is easy to uncover and overcome the limiting beliefs that have been holding you back for so long.

➤ Your earning potential is directly influenced by your self-worth, and you can increase your income significantly by improving your self-value.

➤ True success often has its roots in a previous failure, and your challenges are a springboard that allow you to expand your life and achieve your goals.

➤ Persistence always pays off in a very big way.

➤ Your mind and body influence each other profoundly, and by improving your health, you can increase your brain power, and create greater happiness and fulfilment in your life.

➤ You can use high performance techniques to speed up your progress, reduce your stress, and gain more energy and freedom.

> ➤ Mentors, coaches, and mastermind groups can dramatically speed up the achievement of your goals, and are the "hidden secret" of highly successful people.

> ➤ Discovering your own unique life purpose is not difficult, and you can use it to create greater success, happiness, and fulfilment – and it can help you to achieve your life's biggest goals.

> ➤ Time is your most valuable possession, and when you use it wisely, you can achieve more in a single day than most people achieve in months.

> ➤ You have a "hidden inner genius" that you can use to get answers to your problems, and to unlock unlimited creativity.

Your New Life

My hope is that while you have been reading this book, you will have become a lot more aware of how your own mind operates, and that you will also have started to see how you have been holding yourself back from success in many different ways.

If you have completed the exercises to uncover your limiting beliefs in step 7, then I believe you will already be quite shocked by the extent to which you have been sabotaging your own goals. If for any reason, you have not done that exercise yet, then please do it immediately after you have finished reading this book.

Becoming aware of and overcoming your limiting beliefs is one of the most powerful things you can do during your lifetime, because it has the power to transform every area of your life and empower you like never before. As I mentioned earlier, it's a bit like being reborn. By sweeping the slate clean and starting afresh without any impediments in your way, you will discover that what was difficult before is now a lot easier, and you will be able to achieve whatever you want from now on.

When you start stretching your life beyond your existing comfort zone and start experiencing challenges, you will start to feel more engaged with life. And when you push yourself towards a brighter, happier, and more fulling future, it will light up your heart and soul and imbue you with energy and vitality. Then you will start to feel more alive than ever before.

Do's and Don'ts

Here are some important steps you must take right away, as well as several things you need to avoid:

- ➤ **DO** - get started immediately and don't delay
- ➤ **DO** - read through the 7 steps several times
- ➤ **DO** - every exercise in this book
- ➤ **DO** - use the Daily Success Planner every day
- ➤ **DO** - reprogram your mind daily
- ➤ **DO** - get the free gift included with this book

- ➤ <u>Don't</u> – procrastinate – get started right away!
- ➤ <u>Don't</u> – set big short-term goals
- ➤ <u>Don't</u> – allow yourself to be defeated by temporary setbacks
- ➤ <u>Don't</u> – listen to your negative inner voice
- ➤ <u>Don't</u> – allow anyone to influence you negatively
- ➤ <u>Don't</u> – berate yourself, as it slows down your progress
- ➤ <u>Don't</u> – ever give up!!!

It's Time for You to Decide

Your current circumstances never define who you are, what you can achieve, or who you can become. You have everything within you right now to be wildly successful and deeply happy on a long-term basis.

However, at this point you need to make a choice – you can either continue doing what you have always done and continue getting the results you have always got or you can take action immediately on what you have learned in this book. All you need do is take one first step, and then another and another. And before long you will be amazed by just how far you have come and how much you have achieved.

With this simple seven step system you can become empowered, successful, and happy, and achieve all your goals – fast! Do not put this book on the shelf to just gather dust. Keep it close to you all the time, and use it as your reference guide - so you start living the life you were born to live.

Get started right away with <u>my free training on the next page</u>, and continue your learning by checking out my products and coaching programs on the pages after that.

I wish you great success in everything you do, and a deeply happy, fulfilling life, where you achieve all your life's biggest goals.

Very best wishes,

Mike Pettigrew
www.MikePettigrew.com

Your Free Gift

As a way of saying thank you for purchasing this book, I'm offering you a free webinar that covers many of the ground-breaking strategies you have discovered in these pages. In "10 Easy Steps to Achieve Anything You Desire", you will learn how to achieve your goals 10 times faster, and how to achieve a life of success, empowerment, and happiness.

You will learn how to:

➤ Achieve any goal 10 times faster
➤ Accomplish more in the next 12 months than in the last 12 years
➤ Overcome every block holding you back
➤ Attract success, happiness, and wealth into your life
➤ Be motivated and empowered to achieve all your goals

You will also learn how to quickly and easily change negative thoughts and emotions, and how to reprogram your mind for success and happiness.

This high content free webinar reveals the exact steps that will lead you to a life of happiness, success, and fulfilment, and it acts as your companion to this book. The webinar runs daily and there is a very *special offer for you right at the end.*

10 Easy Steps to Achieve Anything You Desire
Get this FREE training now:
www.mikepettigrew.com/10steps

Products and Coaching Programs
available from the author

The 30 Day Success Formula

Can You Really Become Successful in Just 30 Days? - with this 6-CD audio program you just might find its possible!

What if I told you that within the next 30 days, you could...

- Get crystal clear on exactly what you want from life and your true purpose
- Overcome obstacles that have been stopping you from achieving your goals
- Start dramatically improving all areas of your life
- Create a simple effective plan to accomplish all your goals

Would you go for it? Would you take the opportunity to create a much better life for yourself? Here's your chance to do this.

Achieve your life's biggest dreams and *enhance every area of your life:*

- **Become successful** & achieve what you want
- *Feel happier* & more empowered
- **Develop greater confidence**
- Experience a richer and *more fulfilling life*

"Mike's programme is one of the most authentic and purposeful products I have experienced."

Dr Linda Mallory, Educational Psychologist

Just 30 Days to a New Improved You!

More details: www.mikepettigrew.com/30day

The Millionaire Mind Secrets

The Astonishing System that Creates the Mind of a Millionaire – even if you are currently broke or unemployed.

In this 73-page eBook and audiobook you will learn how millionaires think, so you can model their success. It's about more than just wealth creation, and there's an optional upgrade that includes a full success mindset programming toolkit.

This special mind programming toolkit includes: hypnosis recordings, subliminal software and audio tracks, binaural beats and training videos.

Here's just a fraction of what you're getting...

- **The truth about how wealth is created,** and why it's got nothing to do with hard work! Learn the true causes of success and wealth, so you can create whatever you want from now on. Page 6.

- **Learn how millionaires think, and model their success** - so you don't have to reinvent the wheel. Millionaires think very differently to most people, and when you start copying their thought processes, you open the door to unlimited possibilities. Page 67.

- *Money doesn't grow on trees* - **BUT it does grow in your mind.** Learn how to create the millionaire mindset, so you can *do more of what you love.* Page 59.

- **5 Powerful Mind Programming Tools** - simple yet amazing short-cuts you can take to *quickly create a millionaire mindset and a more fulling life.* Page 17.

"Mike's program is a great source of inspiration. It has helped me to be more empowered to achieve my goals."

Inese Kapeniese Consultant, Coach and Author

More details: www.themillioinaremindsecrets.com

Ultimate Success Club Group Coaching

Ultimate Success Club – a life changing membership program for those who want to achieve all their goals faster

Most highly successful people use a coach, to help them to go beyond their current limitations and to reach their life's biggest goals.

Coaching will help you to achieve far more than ever before and it's the "hidden" secret of the world's most successful people and all high achievers.

Just some of the many benefits of this coaching program...

* Helps you **create a clear vision** of what you want in your life
* *Creates a plan of action,* so you can **achieve your goals faster**
* **Helps improve your self-worth,** and *gives you greater confidence*
* Enables you to find new options and perspectives to choose from
* Enables you to **become more motivated and empowered**
* Helps you stay accountable and on-track
* Enables you to **use your time more effectively** *and productively*
* Helps identify and overcome barriers to your progress
* Allows you to *live a more balanced, richer and fuller life*
* Enables you to **achieve everything you want from life**

Your monthly membership includes 2 one-hour group coaching sessions each month by webinar where you can also ask Mike anything.

In addition, you will get **complimentary access to some of Mike's best products**, courses and training, added to your membership each month.

More details: www.mikepettigrew.com/special

Certified High Performance Coaching

High Performance Coaching is a revolutionary form of coaching that allows you to excel and succeed above standard norms over the long-term.

Even if you are already very successful, there will be times when you feel tired, and lack enthusiasm or motivation. It's easy to settle for mediocrity, even though *you know in your heart that there is so much more.*

High performance coaching is **structured differently to all other forms of coaching,** and it takes you through a process that has been proved scientifically to work.

Every session has *an outcome that moves you towards high performance,* no matter what's going on in your world.

This means **you become better in all areas of your life,** and you have greater abundance, fulfilment, aliveness and joy, with *a sustained ability to be "in flow".*

This is probably the most effective type of coaching in the world, with **a satisfaction rating of 94%** (from over 30,000 sessions), compared to most other forms of coaching that have a satisfaction rating of between 60% and 80%.

To become a real high performer and **to achieve at the top levels** you need a coach who has a plan for you to lift your life in a holistic way.

Mike is one of only 300 Certified High Performance Coaches in the world, and he will share with you advanced tools and strategies so you **become more productive, influential, and successful** and *achieve your goals more easily.*

Always limited availability, and by application only – it also includes membership to the Ultimate Success Club group coaching program.

More details: www.mikepettigrew.com/chpc

Review Request

You probably already know how important good reviews are for the success of books like this on Amazon.

If you enjoyed this book or if you found it helpful, then I'd be very grateful if you would post a positive review. Your support really does matter and it makes a big difference by helping other people. Of course, I read every review so I can get your feedback.

To leave a review, all you need to do is go to the review section on this book's Amazon page. You will see a big button that says, "Write a customer review" – just click that button and you can start writing your review.

Here is a URL that will bring you there:

www.mikepettigrew.com/gasreview

Again, thank you for your support.

Very best wishes,

Mike Pettigrew

Affirmation Library

The 357 affirmations included here are provided as a reference guide and starting point for creating your own affirmations. You can use them as templates for creating those affirmations. Although you can use them exactly as they are, **you will get far better best results** <u>when you convert your own condensed goals into affirmations</u> as explained in step four of this book.

If you are using a subliminal program on your computer while you are working, you may find some of these helpful. However, always create and use your own affirmations for best results!

Confidence:
My mind is strong and powerful
I am self-confident
I can do anything I set my mind to
I have confidence
I am charismatic
I am upbeat
I am passionate
I handle situations easily
I am the master of my emotions
I can relax in every situation
There is nothing I cannot handle well
I think wisely
I am more in control each day
I have peace of mind
I have a strong mind

I create thoughts that bring me peace
I have a high state of tolerance
I am bigger than any problem

Creativity:
I easily tap into my creativity
I am very creative
My creativity is boundless
I am creative and productive
I allow creativity to flow through me
I have hundreds of excellent ideas
My creativity brings me wealth, success and recognition
I easily connect with my infinite creative mind
Creative ideas come to me all of the time
Ideas come easily to me
I can create anything I want
I live in the creative flow of life
I am grateful for my inner genius and creativity
I have infinite creativity
My imagination is limitless
I have limitless creative potential
I tap into infinite intelligence easily
I Love my creative abilities
I have an endless supply of creativity
I give thanks for the creative ideas that come to me
I have wonderful and creative ideas
It is a joy for me to create
I open up to the flow of creativity
I am intuitive
I trust my intuition
I connect with my inner wisdom easily
My dreams give me guidance
I follow my intuition
I am in touch with my inner self
My intuition grows stronger each day
I listen to my intuition

My hunches turn out to be correct
I am guided by my intuition
Infinite intelligence guides me
My intuition serves me well
I access my intuition easily
My inner wisdom guides me perfectly

Goals & Productivity:
My goals come to fruition
My mind is focused
I am an amazing success
I am a powerful creator
I always make the right decisions
I get what I want
I know exactly what I want
I achieve all I want
I am congratulated for my achievements
I am appreciated, acknowledged, and admired for my amazing
    productivity
I achieve my goals and live my dreams
I know what I want
I achieve my goals
Every day in every way I am more productive and efficient
I produce more and more in less time
I am achieving all my goals
I can achieve anything
What I believe in I achieve
I know exactly what I want and I get what I want
I am focused and productive
I have total concentration
I always complete my tasks rapidly, superbly and efficiently

Happiness:
I live each day with passion
I deserve to be happy
I am full of joy and happiness

I love life and myself
My happiness is reflected in my smile
My pleasing personality is contagious
I am joyful about each new day
My happiness comes from within me
I choose happiness now!
My happiness continually brings me more happiness
I am always kind and thoughtful towards to others
My sense of humour touches everyone around me
I choose to be happy at the start of each day
I choose health and happiness
My joy brings blessings into my Life
I attract joy into my life
I live life with passion and enthusiasm
Life is fun
I love life
I create my own happiness
My future is brighter than ever

Healing:
My powerful mind heals my body
Every cell in my body vibrates with health
My body heals as I sleep
I am strong, healthy and pain free
Each day I become more and more pain free
I release any pain in my life NOW
I am strong physically, emotionally and mentally
I am pain free
I can feel my body becoming stronger
I am grateful for my healing
The root cause of my pain heals now
I know that my healing is already in process
I am healthy, healed and whole
My body heals quickly and easily

Health & Exercise:
I love to exercise
I exercise regularly
Exercise makes me healthy
Exercise revitalizes me
I exercise more and more each week
Exercise makes me feel great
I find time to exercise
Exercise gives me lots of energy
I am a perfect example of health
My fitness routine is enjoyable
I feel healthier and healthier each day
My exercise routine yields great results
I exercise and it shows

Listening & Communication:
I am a good listener
I smile often
I use encouragement
I can easily see the other person's point of view
I respect other people's opinions
I use names whenever possible
I am sincere and honest
I am sympathetic to other points of view
I am genuinely interested in other people
I make others feel important
I deeply respect others
I give positive reinforcement
I admit my mistakes quickly
I am tolerant
I give sincere compliments
I am friendly
I am honest
I praise improvement
I begin in a friendly way
I am a great listener

Marriage:

My marriage grows more loving each day
I am loyal and devoted to my partner
I am happily married
My marriage brings a lifetime of happiness
My marriage is built on love, loyalty, and trust
I am passionately in love
I am happier and more in love every day
I am deeply in love with my partner
I am in a perfect and loving marriage
I am grateful for my beautiful and loving marriage
I deserve love and happiness
I give and receive love generously

Memory & Focus:

I focus easily
I remember facts easily
My memory serves me well
I remember more each day
I remember the names of people I meet
I remember what I read
My memory improves each day
I am a memory master
I remember the things I see
I remember easily and effortlessly
I remember what I learn
My memory is perfect
I am grateful for my excellent memory
I have a photographic memory
I have excellent recall

Parenting & Children:

I am a great parent
I am a supportive parent
I listen to my children attentively
I deeply respect my children

I support my children always
I allow my children freedom
I show my children unconditional love
I give my children positive encouragement
I teach my children care and respect for others
I teach my children through my example
I allow my children to dream BIG
I keep my promises to my children
I love my children
I praise my children often
I am proud of my children and tell them
I have fun with your children
I am always there when my children need me

Positivity:
I have a positive outlook on life
I am a positive person
I think positive
I am grateful for everything
I am in control
I am generous
I am grateful for all the good in my life
I fill my mind with beautiful thoughts
I am the creator of my experience
I always focus on the positive
I have a positive mindset
I surround myself with positive people
I see the good all things
I believe in myself
I am a winner
I find the gift in every experience
I become more positive each day
I am in control of my mind
I am passionate about life
I am open to giving to others
I enjoy the overflowing abundance in my life

Public Speaking:

I love speaking in public

I am confident when speaking

I am an excellent speaker

I am an inspiring speaker

I am an engaging and enthusiastic speaker

I am passionate about speaking

I speak from my heart

I have valuable information to share

I handle questions easily

My audience loves me

My audience appreciates me

I interact well with groups

I give excellent presentations

I make eye contact with my audience

I am well prepared when speaking

My presentations are always clear

I say exactly the right things

Releasing Past Hurt:

I let go of the past

I move forward in life happily

I forgive and forget

I forgive myself and others

I move forward towards greater good

I am thankful for my wonderful future

I find closure and move on with my life happily

I look to a better future

The past has no power over me

You now release old hurt

I now release anger and resentment

I gracefully release my past

Self-Acceptance:

I am wonderful just the way I am

I possess beauty and strength

I treat my body with love and respect
I am blessed with many talents
I look at the beauty life has to offer
I see the wonderful person I am
I treat myself with deep respect
I accept and embrace myself
I am a caring person and loved by many
I deserve the love of others

Self-Esteem:
I have sky-high self-esteem
I am a high achiever
I am worthy
I love myself
I am Awesome
I approve of myself and feel great
I value myself
I look people in the eyes
I am a worthwhile person
I am worth all my hearts desires
People like me
I am charming
I get along well with others
I have personal magnetism
My personality is appealing
I have a pleasing personality
I am fun
I am witty
People find me fascinating
Others are attracted to me
I am likeable
My charming personality draws others to me
I connect with others easily
I have courage
I have self control

Success:

I am happy, successful, and fulfilled

I deserve to be prosperous and successful

Success is my birthright and I accept it now

I am successful in all areas of my life

I am successful

I am the creator of my experiences

I was born to be successful in life

I create my destiny

I give thanks and am grateful for my success

Success comes to me in unexpected ways

I am open to success

I expect success

My will creates my future

I create my life with my vision

I am the master of my destiny

I set my intention and life responds

I accept and deserve success

I know what I want; I ask for it and receive it

Only I hold the key to my destiny

I am success orientated

I have the power to succeed

I celebrate my success

Taking Action:

I take action

I make definite decisions

I take responsibility for my actions

I come up with practical ideas

I go the extra mile

I am mentally strong

I am a master at details

I delegate tasks effectively

Trust and Patience:

I am a patient person
Each day I become more patient
I take things easy
I can relax when under stress
I take time to enjoy life
No hurry, no worry
I release negative emotions
I am relaxed
I am patient
I know when to let go
I discuss things openly and honestly

Wealth & Opportunity:

I am dedicated to creating wealth
I think and dream BIG
I make millions easily
I play to win
I think like a multi-millionaire
I invest well
I accept and expect wealth
I think in millions, and get what I think
Unlimited income flows in my life
I give thanks for all the money I have
I am a money magnet
I take calculated risks
Everything I touch turns to gold
I make more and more money each year
I see opportunities everywhere
I am NOW accumulating large sums of money
Money comes to me easily and effortlessly
I earn great money doing what I enjoy
I have the Midas touch
I give and receive money with joy
I prosper with everyone I touch

Weight Loss:

I am slim and trim

I am my ideal weight

I am on the road to fitness

I am losing weight now

I lose weight easily

I am enjoying how I'm feeling now

I am careful about what I eat

I am feeling slimmer today

I only eat healthy foods

I am getting fitter every day

I am getting slimmer and healthier

I enjoy my healthy lifestyle

I look and feel lighter today

I love the feeling of making progress

I love food that makes me slim

Losing weight is effortless

Losing weight is easy!

I love being healthy

I only eat when I need to

I exercise frequently

I have a fast metabolism

References

Andrew Carnegie. *Who is the richest person to ever have lived?* (inflation-adjusted), Quora.

Benjamin Baird and Jonathan Schooler. *Mind Wandering Facilitates Creative Incubation*. University of California, Santa Barbara. August 31st, 2012.

Brendon Burchard. *High Performance Academy. High Performance Habits*. 2017. 10 Steps to Achieving Anything 10X Faster.

Thomas Budzynski, Ph. D. *The Clinical Guide to Sound and Light*. 1990.

Carl Benedikt Frey & Michael Osborne. *The Future of Employment*. University of Oxford. September 13th, 2013.

Gary Keller and Jay Papasan. *The One Thing*. April 1st, 2013.

Harold Russell, Ph.D. At the 1991 AAPB (Association of Applied Psychophysiology and Biofeedback) Annual Meeting in Dallas, Texas, *reported on research that showed that light and sound at beta frequencies (18 -21 Hz) appeared to improve the cognitive functioning of ADDH (Attention Deficit Disorder -Hyperactive) children.*

Harvard Medical School. *Sleep and Disease Risk*. December 18, 2007. Sleep and Mental Health. July 2009. Harvard Business Review by Shawn Achor. January 2012. *Harvard Survey of the class of 1980*. 2015.

Jason R. Finley, Aaron S. Benjamin, and Jason S. McCarley. *Metacognition of Multitasking: How Well Do We Predict the Costs of Divided Attention?* Journal of Experimental Psychology. February 3, 2014.

Lissa Rankin M.D. *The Nocebo Effect: Negative Thoughts Can Harm Your Health.* Psychology Today. August 6th, 2013.

Lorenzo Cohen, Ph.D. *A study into the effects of sugar on cancer found that increased consumption of sugar-sweetened beverages is a significant contributor to obesity, heart disease and cancer.* University of Texas MD Anderson Cancer Center. January 2016.

Dr Maxwell Maltz M.D. F.I.C.S. *Psycho-Cybernetics.* 1960.

McKinsey Global Institute. *A Future That Works: Automation, Employment, and Productivity.* January 2017.

Milton, G.W. Self-Willed Death or the Bone-Pointing Syndrome. The Lancet, (23rd June, 1973), pp.1435–1436.

Napoleon Hill. *Think and Grow Rich.* 1930.

Nichiren. *"first of all learn about death, and then about other things".* Major Writings of Nichiren Daishonin. Volume 2, P297.

Nielsen Total Audience report. June 2016. *Showed that on average, American adults are watching five hours and four minutes of television per day.*

Othmer, S & Othmer, S.F. EEG *Training for ADHD and Learning Disorders.* March, 1989.

Pim van Lommel, Cardiologist. *Near-death experience in survivors of cardiac arrest: a prospective study in the Netherlands.* The Lancet. December 15th, 2001.

Quanhe Yang, PhD. *Study published by JAMA Internal Medicine.* November 6th, 2013.

Dr Raymond Mood. *Life After Life.* 1975.

Dr Sam Parnia. *AWARE (AWAreness during REsuscitation) study.* University of Southampton.

Weizmann Institute Of Science. *Demonstrated how a beam of electrons was affected solely by the act of being observed.* February 26th issue of Nature (Vol. 391, pp. 871-874).

Zig Zigler. *"There are no traffic jams on the extra mile".*

31465378R00146

Made in the USA
Middletown, DE
01 January 2019